IF IT DOESN'T GO UP DON'T BUY IT !

How to Make 30% to 50% Annually With Your Mutual Funds Working One Hour a Month

Al Thomas

First Edition
1st Printing 1999
2nd Printing 2000

WILLIAMSBURG INVESTMENT COMPANY
Merritt Island, Florida

"Beware of experts. You don't need a shoemaker to know your shoes fit tight."
    –Leo Tolstoy

"Only misconceptions need to be supported by elaborate arguments. Truth can always stand alone."
    –Shantidasa

Library of Congress Cataloging-in-Publication Data
ISBN-0-9671553-0-4
TXu 834-531

*This book is for
my wife and lover, Carolyn,
so she won't have to listen to
all the bad advice I know she will get
when I am gone,
and
for all the little investors
who are getting bad advice now.*

Acknowledgements

To my good friend, *Ed Gimzek,* for all his help and advice. I could not have put this together without him. Writing was the easy part. Getting it to press was a grizzly. Ed's knowledge of marketing is formidable.

To *Beryl Wolk,* another marketing genius, who continues to push and pull me into new and unknown territories.

To *Glenn Smith,* my brother-in-law and great fisherman, who took the time to carefully edit my first raw manuscript.

Contents

Introduction

This is not a get-rich-quick-scheme book. It is written for the little guy with a few thousand dollars or more who is putting away cash for retirement, the person who is adding monthly to his/her (the last politically correct reference you will find here) IRA or other tax-deferred plan, for those who have college accounts for the kids and especially for you retired folks.

This is a slow, steady, safe way to average 30% to 50% annually over any five-year period with your money or to live more comfortably on the nest egg you have now. This advice will keep you out of every major bear market.

Every professional trader knows that the first rule of investing is to protect your capital. I am *not* going to train you to be a trader. Absolutely not! I will just show you how you can easily *double your money every three or four years* and keep from losing it when the brown stuff hits the blades. You will have to review your portfolio once a month for a few minutes, but that's easy.

This is the most outrageous book you will ever read on how to make money in mutual funds, stocks, futures or options. I trash all the brokerage houses, brokers, mutual fund managers, economists, money managers, bankers and every analyst who ever drew a breath... and a lot more. And when I say trashed, I mean that for a change you will be reading the truth. You'll never hear my being interviewed on radio or TV talk shows because I step on every toe that has big money. I am a pariah to the industry. Only to the small investor, you, can I be a hero.

There are literally thousands of ways to invest your money from real estate to collectibles; millions of ways of trading whatever venue you choose.

I haven't seen them all, but I have seen many and tried hundreds. This book distills the best of what I have seen and some of what I have learned about trading in the financial markets over the last 30 plus years. If I knew then what I know now and had applied it, I'd easily be a multimillionaire. Depending on your age when you do apply what you will learn here, you can become rich or at least live more comfortably on what you have.

First, let's find out if this book is for you. Maybe you shouldn't buy it or maybe you ought to take it back before you get it dirty because I am going to smash some idols, strangle some pet strategies and be totally irreverent about Wall Street theories. And I'm going to 'throw-up' on many of your business friends — especially your broker. But you will make a lot of money and ultimately have the last laugh (all the way to the bank). This was not written for those guys on Wall Street, although at least 90% don't know what I am going to tell you. Even if they did, they definitely would not tell you. To them, making 10% to 20% per year on your money is excellent, fantastic, great.

I say, "Hooey!" (They won't let me print what I really want to say). You can do better and you definitely don't need them.

Conventional wisdom on Wall Street says making 12 to 15% is wonderful. Let me explain what conventional wisdom really is; it is conventional stupidity, it is tunnel vision. It means they don't know how to do better. You can average 30% to 40% annually over any five-year period of time.

Are you a *trader* or an *investor*? Do you have an *investment plan*? Is your trading *conservative* or *aggressive*? And what the heck does that mean anyway? These terms are all part of the smoke and mirrors created by the investment community—brokerage houses, investment bankers, banks, financial planners, etc. These terms are used to make the little guy (you) with a little money (that's under a million dollars to the pros) think you are really getting the best advice on where to invest your money. You are *not*.

Basically, we all want to have our money working for us in stocks, bonds, real estate, commodities, collectibles, etc. We want to get rich. Everybody loves money. In this book, I will show you many ways to get rich, but more than that, I will show you how to protect what you have already made. I will caution you *not* to do most of the dumb things the 'experts' want you to do. This book is primarily for plain folks who don't have financial advisers, but who want to safely make money in mutual funds. Almost all the advice you get from brokers, financial planners and bankers is bad — and I'll prove it to you as you read along.

We have been told a trader is a *shooter* — some wild speculator who is buying and selling every day. You are never going to do that and I sure agree that is *not* what you want to do. And it is not what I want you to do. But, did it ever occur to you that an investor is just a long-term speculator? Yes, you *are* a speculator — even you nice little old ladies with the three-wheel bicycles and you old guys with the walkers. I bet you thought an "investor" was one of those conservative people who knows all about PE ratios, book value, insider trading, etc., etc.... who wears a suit and tie every day, and studies his portfolio with the Wall Street Journal at his side. You know, a kind of aloof *know-it-all!* It might just be some lady who looks at the investment page in the paper occasionally (like my mother-in-law) to see how her stocks and mutual funds are doing. No, an "investor" is no different from a *shooter* — only the time frame is different. Your broker wants you to think you are one of those "long term" investors because when the market starts down he can say, "you are in for the long haul" while you watch your account get smaller and smaller every day. If you want to have any money at the end of the "long haul", you'd better pay attention to what I have to say. Don't think otherwise or you are just kidding yourself.

Anyway, you want to make money and I want to give you some honest information that no broker, banker, brokerage firm or investment adviser will give you because it will make him look bad and he won't make any commission. Say, maybe *that's why they won't tell you.* He will tell you he only believes in "conservative investments". That is an oxymoron. *There is no such thing as a conservative investment.* That's kind of like an "honest politician" or "military intelligence". Remember that blue chip stock — Pan American Airways? The 'buy-and-hold' guys are still holding it in that dark place.

Before you hire a financial adviser, insist he read this book. If you already have a financial adviser, insist he read the book or you will take your business elsewhere. It will be interesting to hear his criticisms and excuses. Let me know what he says. Just a little common sense will show he is either lying or stupid and you don't want him if he is either. If he agrees, please hang on to him — you have a jewel. Now make him perform! The only reason you might want to pay him is because you can't "pull the trigger" when you get a signal. He will do it for you automatically. He will be worth his fee. That will be his only function. No advice, no recommendations, nothing. And have him reduce his fee since you don't want his "expertise"

When your broker tells you he is *conservative*, it really means **he** is willing to settle for less return on **your** money. What I am going to show is conservative because you will be buying mutual funds that go up and you won't be in the market when it's going down. *Safety* and *performance* are my two key watchwords.

Basically, I am talking about 'Market Timing' versus 'Buy-and-Hold'. We haven't had a major break in the market for the last 10 years. The 1987 crash lost about 33% and even that one got you "even" in about 2 years. The recent "correction" in the latter half of 1998 took the market down 20% and it came back up to "even" in just a few months. With the method I will show you in the following pages, you would have been out of the market from the beginning of August and have gotten back into it the first week of November, so you would not have had to sweat out that terrible break. You could have slept like a baby while all your friends were pacing the floor all night long.

Because we have had such a long and sustained rise, the 'Buy-and-Hold' strategy *seems* to be working. Just shut your eyes. My broker says, "the market always comes back", but it may take a lifetime. Can you wait that long? Brokers are taught not to sell, especially near the top. And they definitely don't want you to have cash in your account; you might take it out. There is too much historical evidence that proves Buy-and-Hold does *not* work. Market timing is a must if you not only wish to make money but wish to preserve your capital through the next downturn. This especially applies to you retired folks.

Since the turn of the century — almost 100 years — there have been about 30 "corrections" or bear markets averaging *more* than 32% each. Nine of these averaged almost 50%. Do you want to buy-and-hold through the next one? *There will be one!* The *Kiplinger Personal Finance Magazine* in 1997 found that from 1972 to 1997, market timing outperformed and avoided the worst market crashes of 1973-74, 1987 and 1990.

Even the Federal Reserve Board printed an article in 1997 under the title, *Earnings Forecasts and the Predictability of Stock Returns; Evidence from Trading the S&P500* in which they concluded, "the rule produces superior returns, both relative to those earned under buying and holding the S&P and the relative market timing implementations". That's Fed talk for market timing outperforms Buy-and-Hold.

The Buy-and-Hold crowd believes there is safety in utility stocks. Your broker probably also believes this great myth. From the crash high in October 1929 it took until 1942 for the utility index to reach the old high — 13 years. During the break in 1973-74 the utility index sank to 60% below the 1929 highs and it wasn't until the late 1980s that the index made a new high. Do you still want to buy and hold? I don't. Never keep your money in a losing position. There are other places where you can be making a good return. I'll show you how.

If you received a 15% return compounded for 10 years on $10,000 you would have over $40,000. But suppose you ran into a 50% decline? Your money would drop to $20,000. That hurts!

A Buy-and-Hold strategist is guaranteed to lose in every one of these declines. Believe me, you won't have to wait 10 years for the next one.

Successful investing does not mean catching the occasional, short term, hot stock that runs from 2 to 102. *Smart investing is the reduction of risk while focusing on steady long-term profits.*

Markets are orderly. Anyone who believes the market is chaotic is using aboriginal thinking. It is a linear cycle that keeps repeating itself over and over again. The chaotic theory of the market does not see the linkage of the psychology of people and time. Everything in this continuum from the smallest subatomic particle to the galaxies has an orderly pattern. It is up to you to understand it. Once you see it it then becomes predictable and you can use it as a tool.

Any time you put your money into a situation where you are not in complete control, you are speculating; you must not allow anyone to make decisions for you.

I will show you how to step carefully so you won't go over the cliff.

Reprinted with permission

You don't want to get "even". You want to get rich.

You can fool some of the people all of the time and all of the people some of the time, but you can't fool all of the people all of the time. However, the investment industry has been coming as close to the latter as any group I know of. It is about time you got unfooled.

Read on.

Mutual Funds

A mutual fund as we discuss it here is a trust or corporation formed to purchase securities with funds provided by individuals or other entities. The idea is to have a professional analyst select many different stocks to diversify risk. There may be as few as a dozen issues (stocks) or as many as several hundred depending on the philosophy of the fund manager. He may specialize (look for a particular type of stock or region of the world in which to invest) or diversify (buy anything and everything) as he deems its value for appreciation or return (dividend pay-out).

This is the most important section in the book for everyone. I am going to show you how you can earn *2% to 5% per month or more* on your mutual funds and you don't need a broker to do it. In fact, you definitely don't want one as he will interfere. You will not earn that every month, but you can average 30%, 40%, even 50% annually over any 5-year period.

As you will find out, I am death on most brokers because they are not trained to make you money (and most do not realize this). Most are honest guys who have been trained to make commissions because that is how they, and the house, get paid. *Merrill Lynch, Paine Webber* and every other brokerage house in the world is not there to help you get rich. They are there to get rich off you. If you happen to make some money while they are doing it, they are willing to take credit for the 'expertise' they have provided.

You and your broker have been mesmerized by being told you must do *"research and study companies, learn all about them before you invest"*. Don't bother. Total nonsense. Whatever you find out is merely window dressing and doesn't mean anything to your bottom line. What really counts is after you buy it does it go UP? Any stock or mutual fund you buy that goes up is a 'blue chip'. All the rest are dogs.

So far you have been a good student. The brokerage firms, financial planners, bankers, advisers, etc. have been the teachers. Read those prospectuses, study the Price/Earnings (PE) ratios, scrutinize the balance sheets, etc., etc. Unfortunately for you, they are BAD teachers.

There is one basic rule for mutual funds — if your fund is not outperforming the S&P 500 Index sell it immediately and buy a fund that is. Period. End of story. I'll show you how.

> **NEVER** buy a mutual fund that is in a downtrend
> **NEVER** average down.
> **NEVER** pay large commissions, if any.
> **NEVER** try to pick the bottom! Or the top!

The *Standard & Poor's 500 Index*, usually referred to as the "S&P", is the yardstick of the market. It is a market average composed of 500 stocks on the New York Stock Exchange (NYSE). Some are very large corporations, some are relatively small. For our discussion it doesn't matter. It is accepted as what 'the market' as a whole is doing — going up, down or sideways.

You don't have to do any research at all. None. Zip. Nada. Why? Because you are going to hire several of the best analysts on Wall Street to work for you. Free. Yep, free! Don't try to select an individual stock by yourself. First of all, you probably don't know how and second, any information you can get is already reflected in the stock price. You might think you don't have enough money to do this, but all you need is $500, $1,000 or $2,500 total investment funds and you can hire the top guns that are outperforming the market. How?

They are the mutual fund managers. These guys are paid seven figures to manage all the money in the fund; you get the benefit of their expertise no matter how little you might have in that fund. It is their job to do the 'research' to determine whether or not to buy or sell certain stocks. They work 60 and 80 hours per week and never really stop thinking about their job. No trader ever has any time off. He is constantly thinking about his stock positions — which ones to buy or sell, add to or lighten up, put on his watch list, etc., etc. His mind never rests. I know. I've been there. And for all those big bucks, over 97% of the mutual funds (there's approximately 10,000 now) don't perform as well as the

Standard & Poor's 500 Index. Would you agree that these fund managers are grossly overpaid? They can't even perform as well as an average. You certainly don't want anyone who is below average handling your money. Do you?

If you were going into the hospital would you want some below average doctor cutting on you? Hardly. You want the best doctor and that applies to a fund manager for your money as well.

One of the great fallacies of mutual fund managers is they have to be as close to 100% invested as possible. That is called keeping your funds working, but it also means they *must* find a stock (even though it might be marginal in their opinion) which they must buy. Sometimes there aren't any. On any given day, over 90% of listed stocks should not be bought. And when their specialized sector fund is headed down they still have to buy because "it is going to come back". But when? Are you going to live that long? You don't have to stay on the rollercoaster with them, do you? Most of them think like "odd lotters" — the little guys who can't afford to buy the full 100 shares called a "round lot".

A very good example of this was in 1997 when the Pacific rim stocks went up for about 3 months and then down for about 6 months to prices below where they started. If the fund manager was smart enough to buy it before it went up, why wasn't he smart enough to sell it before it went down? What happened to all the 'research'? He is supposed to be an expert. He got you in. Why doesn't he get you out? Yeah!

Here are just two mutual funds which you will find listed in almost any major newspaper every day.

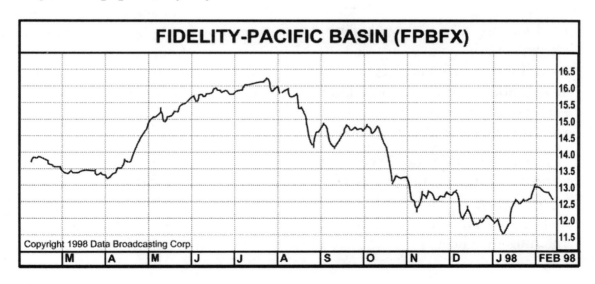

9

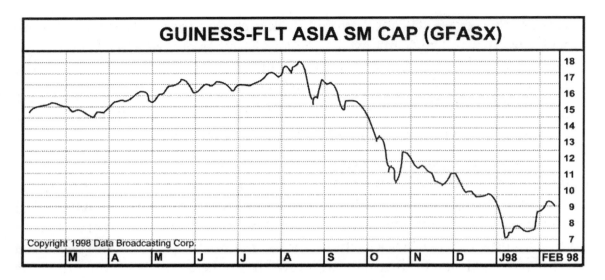

I'm not picking on Fidelity or Guinness here; both have some great performing funds. Their performance, as bad as it was being down 30% to 60% from their highs, was in the same category with all the specialty Pacific funds. What I want to know is "where was the fund manager — out to lunch?" Why wasn't he selling the junk in his portfolio? Because these guys are not taught to sell out bad positions. Buy and hold. Well, it might come back. Hopefully, in their lifetime. Maybe not in yours. Don't you be one of the dummies who lets his money stagnate when you could be in a fund that is making new contract highs every week and definitely outperforming the S&P.

You can't have loyalty to any broker, fund manager or family of funds because they *all* have hot and cold streaks. You must have loyalty to *your* money. Because they don't! I don't know any of these managers, but anyone who does such a bad job with your money should be fired. *Any* fund manager that can't stay close to or exceed the S&P 500 should not have a job! The reason they call themselves analysts is because they are supposed to be able to analyze the direction a stock is supposed to go and when that will happen. Buy and sell. Less than 5% of the fund managers can do it and almost none on a consistent basis. Most of them should be driving taxicabs or working for Roto-Rooter.

Your question should be, "Why do so many funds have a spectacular run up and then lose 50% to 100% of the gain the next year?" The answer is, "Mutual fund managers don't know how to sell". The same is true for stockbrokers in general. See *Upgrades* and *Downgrades* in the Stock chapter — it will have you scratching your head.

Many times I have awakened in the wee hours of the night thinking about positions I had and what to do about them. That was OK, but when I woke up in a cold sweat, I knew I had too many positions. At the opening of the market the next morning I would lighten up to where I could sleep at night. No one trades without emotional involvement when his own money is on the line.

Unfortunately, fund managers are using *your* money.

My friends come to me with their portfolios of mutual funds and stocks and ask me to take a look. Most times I am totally horrified at the poor returns they are receiving. I hear, "My broker said this was a good fund so I bought it 3 or 5 years ago and it has gone up." But how much? Has it kept pace with the S&P 500? In almost every case it has not. Why are you still in the same fund all these years? Haven't you ever heard of rotation? I better explain that one.

But before we get into that, let's take a break and go to the racetrack. Daytona Raceway is nice and I live close by. It's a beautiful day. When we get there the race has already started and we want to place some bets. Darn! Too late. But no, they have just put in a new betting system and they are willing to take our money. (Who isn't?)

You can bet on any car you want and change your bet any time from one to another at the end of each completed lap. Let's see how the race is progressing. Car number 14 did 55 mph and was leading for 37 laps when it came down with engine trouble and fell back to 35 mph. Car 54 found its way to first place with a record 63 mph, but could only sustain it for 18 laps. It then had engine failure and limped into the pit doing 22 mph where they needed a new mechanic to work on the car's performance. Slowly car 87 pulled into the front runner position and managed to maintain a steady performance of 58 mph for 48 laps. He is still chugging along with the top 5 cars. Car 37 just took the lead doing 60 mph, so I am now going to put my money on him.

If you had been in the race from the beginning and kept changing your bet to the lead car you would have been able to have bet on car 14 for 37 laps, car 54 for 18 laps and car 87 for 48 laps. If you had your bet on the leading car for each of the 103 laps your return would be $76 for each dollar you bet for an average of almost $59 each time they went around the track. *If you had not changed your bet your return would have been half that.* You don't need to be a rocket scientist to know that you are not going to keep your bet on a car that dropped from 63 mph to 22 mph just because the driver has a great reputation.

You wouldn't really, would you? Sometimes even the best drivers finish out of the money.

Hey, think about this! Suppose those racing cars were mutual funds and the mph is the annual yield for the mutual funds in your portfolio. Hmm.

But enough time at the track and all that exciting betting. Back to the boring but necessary subject of rotation.

First, let's see if we can have a better understanding of momentum. You are driving along in your car at 55 miles per hour with your foot steadily on the accelerator. As long as you have good gas in the tank, you will continue at the same rate of speed. Uh, oh, your car sputters, maybe you are running low on gas. What happens? You slow down, of course. The same principle applies to mutual funds except that the fuel is the good stocks in that fund. A "good" stock is one that goes up after you buy it. If the stocks in the fund begin to lose their upward movement it is just the same as running out of gas. The fund slows its upward momentum and goes down in value. The fund might even coast along for a while at about the same price (speed), but will be losing value in relationship to other mutual funds which continue to increase in price. Your fund manager is no longer able to find stocks in his sector which fuel the upward price momentum. Time to fill up your tank with a different fuel — switch to another brand of gas, another mutual fund. You are not going to get to grandma's house, retirement, kids college, more income or anything else unless you have good fuel in your tank.

Change in performance of the various mutual funds is something that is occurring all the time; you should be aware of it if you are going to get the best return for your money. Each stock falls into a category or industry group and many have indexes. Many mutual funds are also heavily weighted into industry groups because of their stock portfolios and this is good. There are many indexes that can be tracked. *Worden Brothers Telechart 2000* service has almost 90. *Dow Jones News* has about 125 categories. *Chartcraft/Investor's Business Daily* has about 40 index figures and about 200 industry groups. *Barron's* has another long list.

Most of the stocks within a particular group go up and down at about the same time. There are times when all the technology stocks are rising which could be a few months to over a year. Then they will level off and maybe start down together. Another group such as the oil stocks or the health care category or the bank stocks will become the fastest rising group in the entire market. (Sometimes the fastest falling.) You want to be in the group that is rising fastest because that is where you will make the most money. When that group falters you want to rotate out and go into the group that is now the leader. Just like the auto race. You can do it yourself and you don't need a broker to help you. Read on and I'll make it crystal clear. It's easy.

As I said, because many mutual funds are heavy in a particular category, you want to be in the fund that is moving up faster than the others. They have names like *Technology Fund, Oil Fund, Small Cap Fund, Bond Fund, Large Cap Fund, Bank Fund, Real Estate Fund, Russia Fund* and on and on. Who cares? I just want to make money so, I'll buy the one that is going up fastest and I don't care what they call it.

Kind of like a horse jockey. He doesn't care what the name of his horse is as long as it is the fastest. You are the jockey and your fund is the horse. Never mind the *name* of the mutual fund manager.

Mr. William O'Neil, one of the great market technicians and founder of *Investors' Business Daily* newspaper, did a study which found that between 1953 and 1993, 67% of the move upward in any stock can be credited to the positive advance of the Industry Group and Market Sector to which it belongs. This list is published every day in the *Investor's Business Daily*. You don't need to know this, but if you want to look it up some time that is the place to go. A more recent study shows 49% of the move of any stock is due to the industry group, 31% to the general market movement and 20% to the company itself. This is 'proof' that research is nonsense. Just because the research report on a company is good doesn't mean it is going to go up unless the entire industry group catches fire. Birds of a feather flock together.

You leave the picking of the individual stocks to the mutual fund manager. That is his job. You want the best mutual fund manager on the street *at that time*. You can find him not by name because his name is unimportant, but by performance of his fund. You want the fund that is outperforming all the other funds. You want to get on the 'up escalator' with him and follow him to the top. When he doesn't seem to be able to go any higher, you get off. Take the next escalator up to the higher level following another fund manager. I have no idea who is managing the funds I own and, you know what – I don't care. That is the way I want you to picture the stock market — you, riding gently, easily and steadily up to a level where you get off one mutual fund which has leveled off and choosing another for the ride to the next higher level. That's what rotation is all about.

Remember this one very important fact. Ninety-five percent of all mutual funds do *not* perform better than the S&P 500, which is the bellwether for performance and basically tracks the market. You want to be in the top 1%. And you can! In 1997, only 297 funds out of 8,000 plus outperformed the *S&P 500 Index*. In 1998, according to *Investor's Business Daily* newspaper, there were many more mutual funds to pick from and now you have 319 fund managers who beat the S&P index. Pathetic.

Here is the most important investment advice I can give anyone and I don't care if it is for a new child's college fund or for people who have retired and are living off the income from their savings. Do not pay any attention to that nonsense about living off your dividend return of 5, 6, 7 or 8% because you must have several hundred thousand to a million dollars or more just to maintain your current life style. Most people don't ever save that much; their pension plan won't pay enough either. Don't buy bonds. Don't go into 'conservative' stocks. Don't buy 'defensive' issues. You can consistently earn 30% to 50% annually by being invested with the best performing funds. I'm a heretic. Your broker will hate me, but I will make you money. And you will sleep nights.

STRATEGY

Following this investment strategy should bring you a return of 2% to 5% per *month* while you are in a 'buy' signal — while the market is going up, even sideways, and you will *never* have a major drawdown. It is very simple, but you will have to be disciplined. You will need to review your portfolio *once a month*. It will take less than an hour. That's all!

There is a very simple market-timing device that you can make up and keep yourself, but it takes work and I'm lazy, so I hire others to work for me. I have been fortunate enough to find a couple of gurus who seem to know, at least partly, what they are doing. I'll show you how to coordinate their work so you may substantially increase your profits. And it's easy.

You need to know:

Is the market going up or down?
Which mutual funds should I own?

I subscribe to two market letters (I don't work for these companies and have no affiliation whatsoever other than I subscribe to and pay full price for their service). *Fabian's Maverick Advisor* (800-950-8765) and *No Load Fund*X* (800-763-8639). The total cost for both is about $300 annually. Even a very small account can easily justify this expense, and it is tax deductible. You actually can perform both of their functions on your own because their computations are very simple, but you must willing to spend the time. You don't need to buy their services, but at least call for a free sample. I'm lazy and I pay them to do the work for me.

Fabian's Maverick Advisor has been in the business of timing the market for more than 20 years and they have a real time track record of over 16% per year and *no* major drawdowns. When I say 'timing the market' I mean they tell you exactly *when to sell* and *when to buy*. You will be either 100% invested or totally sold out of every position with your money in a money market account.

Mr. Fabian does not use stops. During extremely volatile markets when the major index is rising at a very steep angle, it is a good idea to have a mental stop-loss for each individual mutual fund of about 10%, maybe more, so you will not be caught in a sudden drastic correction and give back much of your accumulated paper profit.

NoLoad Fund*X tells you *which* mutual funds to buy when you have a buy signal from Maverick Advisor. *Fund*X* ranks about 750 mutual funds every month as to their performance in various categories. It is very simple to pick the best performing funds. There are other places to find good performing mutual funds, but I like the way *Fund*X* does it. Their return over the past 20 years has been about 16% per year. Combining the two methods produces a synergistic effect resulting in a 300% to 400% return on investment.

See NOLOAD FUND*X exhibit.

You will know when to be in the market and which funds to buy or you will be totally cash. Simple.

The *Maverick Advisor* method will have you separate your funds into several parts — domestic funds, international, Asian and gold and others. Pay attention *only* to his *Domestic Fund Composite* (DFC) signals. When the DFC has a buy signal, put 100% of your money into several top performing funds as listed with *No Load Fund*X*. Yep, it's that easy!

July 1999 **NoLOAD FUND★X**

Class 1 - Growth Funds

MOST SPECULATIVE: PRIMARILY STOCK FUNDS SEEKING MAXIMUM CAPITAL APPRECIATION. VERY HIGH RISK AND VOLATILITY.

1	2	3	4	5	6	7	8	9	10	11	12	13	14	15	16	17	18
RANK By Class								TOTAL RETURN WITH REINVESTED DIVIDENDS				NAV(g)	Dividend & Cap Gain Distribs Paid				
This Mo	Last Mo	Fund★X Score	Fund Name	Ticker	Underlying Portfolio	Symbols (See Page 5)	2 Yr to 6/30/99 %	12 Mo to 6/30/99 %	6 Mo to 6/30/99 %	3 Mo to 6/30/99 %	1 Mo to 6/30/99 %	Price Per Share @ 6/30/99	Ex-Date (see i)	Income Dividend	Capital Gain Distribution Date	Short	Long
74	76	- 4.53	AmCen Glbl Gold	BGEIX	Int'l & US gold	OYeAsm	-40	-11.9	- 7.8	- 1.4	3.0	5.06d	6/25/99	0.03	12/97	0.02	0.20
40	34	11.00	AmCen Growth	TWCGX	Lrg estab growth stks	OYeAs	▲ 67	22.9	10.8	3.3	7.0	30.09	12/18/97	0.18	12/98	0.16	5.21
42	29	10.40	AmCen Ultra	TWCUX	Sm-mid cap growth	OYeAs	▲ 60	22.0	12.5	2.0	5.1	37.57	12/19/97	0.20	12/98	-	3.12
36	40	11.80	AmCen Vista	TWCVX	Small-cap growth	OYeIs	1	- 1.2	20.7	17.0	10.7	12.85	12/10/88	0.01	12/97	0.01	0.80
49	57	8.32	Babson Shadow Stk	SHSTX	40% smallest stocks	OYeSs	22	- 0.3	6.9	19.4	7.3	12.06d	6/24/99	0.03	6/99	-	0.30
38	41	11.10	Brandywine	BRWIX	Mid-cap earnings gro	oyA	16	9.5	14.3	11.4	9.2	34.61	10/26/98	0.26	10/98	0.26	0.07
64	56	2.50	Cappiello R Emrg Gro	CREGX	Aggressive small co's	OYeAs	- 5	- 4.4	3.3	8.4	2.7	13.11			12/98	-	0.10
54	48	7.53	Columbia Special	CLSPX	Aggressive small co's	oyeAsb	25	9.9	2.4	10.8	7.0	24.18	12/31/98	0.01	12/98	0.01	-
60	55	3.72	Dreyfus Aggr Gro	DGVAX	Global aggress growth	OYeAs	-40	-13.9	8.7	13.5	6.6	11.41		-	12/98	-	-
53	43	7.93	Federat Min-Cap (Ind)	FMCPX	Russell 2000 Index	OYQsB	21	5.3	7.7	14.7	4.0	14.55d	6/24/99	0.03	11/98	0.04	0.82
**15	10	29.63	Fidelity Aggres Gro	FDEGX	Small emerg gro stks	oyEAsbN	▲110	54.8**	34.0**	12.1	9.6	41.64		-	1/99	0.45	0.27
30	26	14.27	Fidelity Capital Appr	FDCAX	Divers / some global	oyEAsN	49	23.4	17.4	10.7	5.6	25.91	12/30/98	0.09	12/98	-	0.45
26	22	17.80	Fidelity Growth Co	FDGRX	High earnings stk/conv	oyEIsBN	▲ 61	32.6	19.4	9.6	9.6	60.42	12/18/98	0.09	1/99	0.02	0.42
25	14	17.83	Fidelity OTC Portfolio	FOCPX	Over-the-counter stks	oyEAsN	▲ 72	39.9	18.3	7.7	5.4	51.60	12/13/96	0.08	9/98	0.08	1.57
** 6	3	58.38	Firsthand Tech Val	TVFQX	Sector / technology	OYEI	▲ 84	88.5**	66.8**	47.2**	15.0**	53.79	-	-	12/97	1.55	0.57
16	19	26.08	Founders Discovery	FDISX	Small cap <$200m	OYEAsB	▲ 61	33.4	26.4	23.3**	13.2**	30.81	12/26/90	0.10	12/98	-	2.16
**13	12	31.95	Fremont US Mic-Cap	FUSMX	Smallest growth co's	OYEAs	43	40.3	37.2**	31.1**	11.2	28.62	-	-	12/97	-	1.21
51	45	8.00	Heartland Value	HRTVX	Smallest co's / value	OYEAsB	7	- 4.8	11.9	11.7	3.4	32.71	11/3/98	0.06	11/98	-	0.58
** 7	7	44.80	Icon Technology	ICTEX	Sector/ technology	OYEAu	▲ 83	79.5**	42.4**	28.5**	12.8**	18.00	-	-	12/98	0.19	0.60
21	17	19.67	Invesco Dynamics	FIDYX	Technical analysis	OYEAsB	▲ 79	30.4	25.2	14.8	8.3	19.72	4/30/96	0.02	12/98	0.89	0.42
22	16	19.55	Invesco Energy	FSTEX	Sector / energy	OYEAsU	13	4.1	38.0**	22.7**	5.4	13.94	12/11/98	0.00	12/97	0.00	0.04
73	72	- 3.30	Invesco European	FEURX	Sector / Europe	OYEAsUb	31	- 9.0	- 5.6	- 1.6	3.0	16.87	10/30/98	0.01	12/98	0.79	0.90
63	60	3.10	Invesco Fin Svc	FSFSX	Sector/ financial svcs	OYEAsU	42	2.9	5.0	1.3	3.2	30.63	10/30/98	0.25	12/98	-	2.24
72	73	- 1.13	Invesco Gold	FGLDX	Sector/ int'l gold stk	OYEAsUm	-55	- 5.6	- 1.6	0.5	2.2	1.86	12/19/97	0.03	12/98	0.03	-
70	66	0.65	Invesco Health Sci	FHLSX	Sector/ health science	OYEAsU	42	9.5	- 5.1	- 5.8	4.0	57.92	10/30/98	0.13	12/98	0.31	8.54
17	11	24.30	Invesco Leisure	FLISX	Sector / leisure	OYEAsU	▲ 92	41.8**	30.0	15.1	6.3	40.22	12/11/98	0.00	12/98	0.14	1.77
24	50	17.90	Invesco Pacific Basin	FPBSX	Sector / Asia / Pacific	OYEAsb	-37	18.3	20.2	16.2	12.9**	8.69	12/11/98	0.05	12/97	0.05	0.20
28	30	16.05	Invesco Small Co Gro	FIEGX	Emerging gro < $500m	OYEAsB	46	21.1	15.5	16.9	10.7	13.37	5/31/95	0.05	12/98	1.12	0.06
**14	13	30.58	Invesco Tech	FTCHX	Sector / technology	OYEIsU	▲ 74	50.1**	33.5	16.3	14.4**	46.72	12/19/97	0.00	12/97	0.00	1.28
35	21	12.07	Invesco Utilities	FSTUX	Sector / utility stks	OYEQsU	62	24.6	11.4	10.8	1.5	17.96	4/30/99	0.04	12/98	-	0.21
62	71	3.58	Kaufmann	KAUFX	Divers small co's	oyEIsB	7	- 5.3	- 0.5	10.6	9.5	5.65	12/31/87	0.01	11/98	0.01	0.6
68	75	0.83	Lexington Gold	LEXMX	Int'l gold stock / bullion	OYESsBm	-34	- 2.2	- 1.0	2.0	4.5	3.00	9/16/98	0.00	2/84	0.00	-
32	44	13.43	Lexington WW Emerg	LEXGX	Worldwide emerg mkts	OYESsi	-31	4.7	24.7	18.7	5.6	8.89	12/29/98	0.06	12/95	0.06	0.00
** 1	1	119.18	Matthews Korea	MAKOX	So Korea stks	OYEIBi	16	278.5**	85.5**	69.7**	27.0**	7.57	12/27/95	0.08	-	-	-
** 4	5	68.80	Matthews Pac Tiger	MAPTX	So East Asian stks	OYAbi	-14	115.5**	60.7**	60.2**	22.8**	10.97d	6/22/99	0.01	6/98	-	0.06
27	47	16.20	Montgomery Em Mkt	MNEMX	Int'l emerg mkts	OYEAsi	-37	3.9	28.3	21.8	10.8	10.24	12/18/97	0.15	12/97	0.15	0.19
20	23	20.15	Montgomery Glb Com	MNGGX	US & foreign telecom	OYEAsi	▲ 92	31.7	24.8	14.1	10.0	26.73	-	-	12/98	0.49	2.02
69	64	0.73	Montgry Int Sm Cp	MNISX	Both est & emerg mkts	OYEAsi	1	- 3.8	3.9	2.5	0.3	14.55	12/11/98	0.01	12/97	0.01	1.10
50	54	8.13	Montgry Sm Cp (r)	MNSCX	Stks < $600 million	YEAsr	18	- 4.1	9.9	17.2	9.5	16.56	12/18/90	0.02	12/98	0.33	2.44
65	69	2.10	Montgry US Em Gr (r)	MNMCX	Smallest 10% gro stks	OYEAsr	17	- 4.1	- 4.3	10.2	6.6	19.81	11/27/95	0.09	12/98	0.01	1.11
33	59	12.88	Oberweis Emerg Gro	OBEGX	Sm undervalued gro	OYEIB	2	8.2	12.2	13.1	14.0**	26.48	-	-	11/98	-	1.15
59	68	4.45	PBHG Emerging Gro	PBEGX	$10-$250 m gro stks	OYEAsr	1	- 4.1	- 2.5	13.2	11.2	23.34		-	12/98	-	0.08
52	52	7.95	PBHG Growth	PBHGX	Sm gro stks; 50% OTC	OYEIsr	10	0.6	7.0	11.5	12.7	27.34	-	-	12/94	-	0.01
**10	9	40.25	PBHG Tech & Comm	PBTCX	Comm, tech stocks	OYEIs	▲ 86	70.3**	49.6**	15.4	14.9**	31.84	12/29/95	0.00	12/98	-	0.29
23	38	18.83	PIMCo Blair Emg Mkt	PEMIX	Worldwide emerg mkts	oYAsi	-17	11.4	32.6	21.0	10.3	11.22	12/22/98	0.04	12/98	0.05	-
58	51	5.95	Price Financial Serv	PRISX	Sector / financial servs	oyeAU	43	5.3	8.9	6.0	3.6	18.31	12/16/98	0.16	12/98	0.04	0.30
61	62	3.70	Price Health Science	PRHSX	Sector; US & Foreign	oyeAs	30	10.5	- 0.6	- 0.3	5.2	15.91	-	-	12/98	0.22	0.44
41	46	10.90	Price Latin America	PRLAX	Mexico, Cen & So Amer	oAsbi	-24	- 3.8	26.3	15.6	5.5	8.60	12/16/98	0.14	12/96	0.14	-
**11	18	38.03	Price New Asia	PRASX	Pac Basin / no Japan	oyeAsi	-23	55.3**	36.9**	28.0**	15.9**	6.86	12/16/98	0.09	12/96	0.09	-
46	39	8.93	Price New Horiz (r)	PRNHX	Small growth stks	oYeAsr	24	5.8	7.5	15.5	6.9	25.08	12/23/91	0.05	12/98	-	1.27
31	42	13.73	Royce Low-Priced Stk	RYLPX	Small-cap under 15	OYESs	30	1.6	14.4	26.6**	8.3	7.95	-	-	12/98	0.02	0.01
55	67	7.43	Royce Micro-Cap	RYOTX	OTC value stocks	OYESs	13	- 6.6	2.8	22.6**	6.9	8.79	12/10/98	0.00	12/98	0.00	0.50
**12	8	37.55	RS Emer Gr	RSEGX	Small emerging gro	OYEAB	▲115	58.6**	49.6**	17.0	13.0**	34.34	-	-	12/98	0.88	0.00
47	35	8.77	Scudder Develop	SCOVX	Emerging growth stks	OYeAs	32	11.7	11.7	6.6	5.1	42.08	11/17/86	-	12/98	-	0.38
45	63	9.60	Scudder Emg Mkts Gr	SEMGX	Worldwide emg mkts	OYAbi	-23	- 2.8	16.1	16.1	9.0	12.45	12/29/98	0.04	-	-	-
66	74	1.75	Scudder Gold	SCGDX	Gold stock & bullion	OYEIsm	-38	- 4.5	3.6	2.4	5.5	6.35	12/29/98	0.14	12/96	0.14	0.07
44	36	9.98	Scudder Latin Amer	SLAFX	Mexico, Cen & So Amer	OYeAsbi	-16	2.1	23.0	10.7	4.1	21.80	12/29/98	0.37	12/98	-	0.64
** 9	24	40.58	Scudder Pacific Opp	SCOPX	Pacific Rim / no Japan	OYeAsi	-28	49.4**	37.4**	39.7**	19.8**	12.17	12/29/98	0.03	12/93	0.03	-
67	61	1.33	SteinRoe Cap Oppor	SRFCX	Diversified stocks	OYEAs	9	-10.1	3.3	6.3	5.8	30.34	12/21/95	0.01	12/95	0.01	0.99
71	65	- 0.95	Strong Discovery	STDIX	Small cap growth	OYEQs	8	- 5.6	- 5.0	5.5	1.3	16.82	9/27/96	0.24	3/99	0.15	0.07
18	15	20.88	TransAm Prm Agg Gr	TPAGX	Domestic non-diversfd	OYE	x	48.6**	17.4	6.0	7.5	26.31	-	-	-	-	-
** 8	37	43.70	U.S. China Region	USCOX	Mainland & Hong Kong	OyQsbi	-34	37.5	46.5**	50.8**	28.0**	5.58	12/31/97	0.05	-	-	-
56	49	6.65	U.S. Global Resources	PSPFX	Natural resources	OYEAsbi	-33	- 4.1	16.6	12.6	1.5	4.01	12/31/96	0.37	12/98	-	0.2
75	77	-12.13	U.S. World Gold	UNWPX	Gold stock & bullion	OYEAsm	-50	-20.9	-17.0	- 9.5	- 1.1	7.79	12/31/97	0.14	12/88	0.14	0.04
19	20	20.52	USAA Aggressive Gro	USAUX	Emerg growth	Asu	57	32.7	24.0	14.9	10.5	38.06	9/8/94	0.01	9/98	0.01	3.31
34	27	12.80	Value Line Lev Gro	VALLX	Top Value Line ranks	oYeAs	▲ 76	28.3	13.0	2.1	7.8	54.70	12/26/96	0.00	12/98	-	1.21
29	25	15.48	Value Line Spec Sit	VALSX	Top Value Line ranks	oYeAs	▲ 78	25.6	16.3	11.2	8.8	20.59	12/23/97	0.00	12/98	0.34	0.71
** 3	2	70.18	Van Wagoner Em Gr	VWEGX	All size growth co's	OYEAs	▲ 96	118.5**	105.6**	31.9**	12.7	22.53	-	-	-	-	-

6

Reprinted with permission

NoLOAD FUND★X EXHIBIT

Maverick Advisor makes up its own index of several mutual funds called the *Domestic Fund Composite* that he follows without changes. This is not a sensitive signal as it has given only about 20 sell/buy signals over the past 20 years.

Have your account with a discount broker such as *Waterhouse, Quick & Reilly, E-Trade* or *Ameritrade* or any other broker as long as they carry several hundred no load funds and will allow you to trade with *no commission* or *very low commissions*. Also be sure they will *automatically reinvest your dividends and capital gains at no charge*. Sometimes there is a minor charge for switching in less than 90 days. Don't accept a surcharge past 90 days. Trade with a discount broker, as you don't want any stockbroker calling you with recommendations. Discount brokers are not allowed to give stock advice. The best recommendation from a broker is a eulogy for your money. My definition of a broker is a guy who makes you broker.

When *Maverick Advisor* has a BUY signal for its *Domestic Fund Composite*, put ALL (every penny) of your money into mutual funds. Buy signals are not as time sensitive as sell signals. Don't worry about his signals for the *International Fund Composite* or any other composite indexes. Forget these categories as you want to be fully invested in only the best performing mutual funds no matter where in the world they are as listed in *NoLoad Fund*X*. When the United States stock market gets a cold the foreign markets get pneumonia. Stay with the U.S. market signal, their *Domestic Fund Composite*. Actually it really doesn't make any difference whether you are in domestic or foreign funds as long as you remain in the top mutual funds in the first three *Fund*X* categories at all times *except* when you should be totally out of the equity market. This is the most important part of the overall program. Do *not* pick the mutual funds Maverick Advisor recommends.

If you don't wish to subscribe to *Fund*X*, you might want to see the Mutual Fund Section in *Investor's Business Daily*. They list the *Top 25 Growth Funds in Section Two*. Choose the ones that are in the *Last 3 Months* column; any of these are good. Don't worry about the best performers of the last 3 years, that's ancient history. You could actually buy any of the best performing no-load funds and sell them when they fall out of the top 25. It will work and it's cheaper, but you might be making changes more often which is one of the reasons *I do not advocate it*. There is no smoothing of the performance momentum over slightly longer periods of time. The upside is you will be in the current fastest upward movers all the time and you will make more money. Adding one or two or three percentage points is a lot when you are compounding money.

There is another Buy/Sell indicator that I also watch, but it does NOT have the long real-time track record that Investment Resource does. Called the Pitbull Crash Index, it was formulated by W. Henry Ford of the Pitbull Investor. Henry is a super technician and I respect him greatly. It is more sensitive than the Investment Resource signals and sells you out a little sooner, but it is not my primary indicator. These two indicators may not be that far apart with their sell signals so you might wish to wait until they both are in the "Sell" mode. Look on the Internet at **http://www.wwfn.com/crashupdate.html**

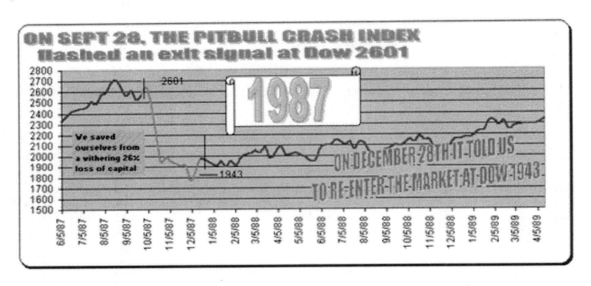

There is going to be another major bear market. I *guarantee* it. It's going to be a mammyjammer. No one knows when. No one knows how severe it will be. I sure as heck don't. A bear market can decline 30% to 50% or more and even if you have the finest mutual funds in the world they *are* going to go *down*. Mutual funds are diversified into many stocks. Like all ships, the stocks go lower when the investment tide goes out. Even the best performing mutual funds decline in a bear market. Get out! Look at the **Market Timing vs. Buy & Hold Exhibit** to see what happened during the 1987 crash.

The regulators have a favorite expression that must appear on all documents — "past performance is no guarantee of future profit". If you had sold near (I didn't say "at") the top, you would be out of the market and earning

MARKET TIMING VS. BUY & HOLD

FUND	OCTOBER 16, 1987					OCTOBER 31, 1987					MARCH 31, 1988			
	SHARES	PRICE	RANK	VALUE	CHANGE	SHARES	PRICE	RANK	VALUE	CHANGE	SHARES	PRICE	RANK	VALUE
Invesco Financial Strategic Pacific	513	$19.49	8	$10,000	None	513	$9.68	25	$4,965	-50%	831	$12.03	4	$10,000
Value Line Leverage Growth	380	$26.33	19	$10,000	None	380	$22.74	18	$8,641	-14%	817	$12.23	51	$10,000
USAA Gold	624	$16.01	1	$10,000	None	624	$10.08	45	$6,289	-37%	1,127	$$8.87	57	$10,000
American Investment Growth	1112	$8.99	10	$10,000	None	1112	$6.04	42	$6,716	-33%	1,628	$6.14	32	$10,000
TOTAL	2,709			$40,000		2,709			$26,605	-33%	4,403			$40,000 + Interest

COMPARISON OF S&P 500

FUND	OCTOBER 16, 1987					OCTOBER 31, 1987					MARCH 31, 1988			
	SHARES	PRICE	RANK	VALUE	CHANGE	SHARES	PRICE	RANK	VALUE	CHANGE	SHARES	PRICE	RANK	VALUE
Vanguard Index 500	352	$28.39		$10,000	None	352	$25.20		$7,954	-20%	390	$25.87		$10,000

NOTES:

Rank is as set forth by NoLoad Fund X.

Investment Resource gave a sell signal on 10/16/87

Investment Resource gave a buy signal in April 1988.

Some funds have slipped to very low rankings, in some cases far below 15. Therefore, you would not want to reinvest in these funds.

interest in your money market account. That interest might not be much, but you would not see your equity disappearing. You would be sleeping well at night while your friends are tossing and turning. When you get the next buy signal you will have a lot more money than you would have had if you held on to your current portfolio.

This is the most important thing you can do is protect your capital as it might take 2 to 5 years or longer to get back to "even" had you not sold. The 1929 crash took more than 25 years to get back to "even".

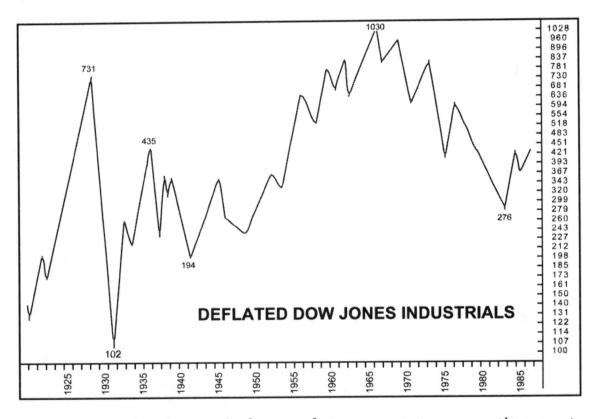

It seems that these major bear markets are one to two generations apart. Why? The reason is very logical and psychological. Once the crowd has been badly stung by the market, "bee people" tend to get out and stay out for the rest of their lives. The experience was too devastating. We have a new bunch of kids now called "boomers", who have not seen a real bear and will more than likely fall into the same trap. They will also get out licking their financial wounds swearing they will never "play the market again". It is their turn to be fleeced. History repeats. To be prepared for the future, you must study the past.

In the 1990's, everyone thought himself to be a financial genius. It was pretty hard not to make money. These investors will be mauled by the next bear. That is why what you are learning here is so valuable. You don't have to be torn apart financially if you will learn and act upon these two simple steps — market timing and intelligent mutual fund selection.

For you who are reading this book after the next crash, I caution you not to turn your back on the market. If you have not heeded my warnings and have lost most of your money, this is no time to withdraw. There are still many good performing mutual funds provided you are in the best performers only when the market is going UP. You can get on the 'up escalator' now to recoup your losses. You should be able to double your investment funds every 3 years. It won't take long to be back on top.

Don't get the idea you will be trading all the time. You won't. The *Maverick Advisor* program has averaged a sell/buy signal only once a year over the past 20 years and they have a real time track record to prove it. They have been right most of the time with their worst drawdown (loss) being only 6%. With the right mutual funds it would not have been that much. They have never had a 20%, 30% or 40% loss like the 'Buy-and-Hold' dummies. Don't think about these signals — ACT immediately. When you get a sell signal call your discount broker. Tell him to sell everything. Cash is king. Put the proceeds in your money market account. Do it!

You should break your funds into 3 or 4 equal dollar units for each part of your investment portfolio so you will be diversified. If you have $100,000 have four $25,000 units. If you have a considerable sum I suggest you still keep it down to not more than 8 or 10 different funds as you don't want to be a slave to your money. This same method of investing also applies to start-up, retirement and children's accounts. With just $5,000 you can still break it into two parts. Have some diversification, but not too much.

There may be a time when you switch from one fund to another and have a loss. That will be very seldom, probably as we are headed into a bear phase of the market. It is like playing poker — you don't win every hand, but you don't keep betting on a hand you know is a loser. Know when to hold 'em and know when to fold 'em. That's what performance shows you in the *Fund*X* service.

If you want to do the work yourself, you can make up your own indexes to provide your own signals which will be different than *Maverick Advisor*. To keep it very simple you could buy the *Investor's Business Daily* to see when the *S&P 500 Index* falls below its 200-day moving average. This must be confirmed by a close below the 200-day moving average of the *IBD Mutual Fund Index*. It will be a pretty good indicator. Check this out by doing a historical study. I haven't done this, but I know it will work. I feel more confident with the use of a dual confirmation of indexes for buy and sell signals.

There is a short cut here if you don't want to pick good mutual funds and are willing to settle for a lot less return on your money. Buy an index fund that mirrors the *S&P 500* almost exactly, such as the *Vanguard Index 500*.

DILBERT by Scott Adams

DILBERT reprinted by permission ot United Feature Syndicate, Inc.

All the major fund families have an index fund of some kind. Put all your money in this and follow the *Maverick Advisor*, or your own "Buy/Sell" signals. This will beat more than 95% of the other mutual funds, but again I must very strongly stress that you must sell and transfer your funds to a money market account when you get a sell signal.

You see the *S&P Index* quoted daily, hourly and almost every minute on CNBC-TV or on the tote board at your broker's office. You don't need to see this every minute. Just follow whatever timing program you like and maybe you will be averaging a signal once a year — sometimes more, sometimes less.

None of these index funds can beat the *S&P 500* because they have expenses charged against the fund causing them to perform very slightly below the *S&P 500*.

Another great Wall Street distraction is who the money manager is for the fund. Who cares? These guys play musical chairs and many people follow them. Why? Hey, so what if you have a bunch of monkeys picking the stocks in the mutual fund portfolio, as long as it is one of the top performers.

DILBERT by Scott Adams

DILBERT reprinted by permission of United Feature Syndicate, Inc.

There are some marvelous mutual fund advisory letters that are constantly being quoted on CNBC-TV, in your daily newspaper financial section and in the various financial magazines.

One of the most quoted is *Morningstar Fund Investor*, a really sophisticated publication. In the September 1998 issue they have a detailed article on "What is...Price/Cash Flow?" as a method of analyzing the valuation of various mutual funds. I guarantee even if you understood it that it will not make you any money. All you need to know is where does the particular mutual fund I own rank in performance among the 8,000 plus funds. If it isn't in the top one percent, you don't want it.

For those of you who are locked into your company's pension plan where they are making contributions, a set amount equal to or partially matching yours, get all of this you can. If you have to buy company stock you're screwed; it may or may not be a good deal. Many companies allow you to invest your contributions in a family of funds like *Invesco* or *Loomis* or *Fidelity*, which is fine. As part of all fund families there is usually a plain vanilla money market fund. Just transfer all your funds to that one when you get a sell signal. I'll show you how to pick the best from that family of funds later on when you get a buy signal. *NoLoad Fund*X* does list many *Fidelity Funds*. I don't select any *Fidelity Funds* because they will charge me a first time commission to trade and there are hundreds of good no load (no commission) funds out there which I might choose that are just as good or better.

There are thousands of mutual funds, and less than 5% are worthwhile, but which ones? Again, I'm lazy so I pay someone else to do the work for me. The market letter from *NoLoad Fund*X* will guide you very clearly; they have been in business for 20 years. They grade funds by performance and score each one. Choose a fund that has a ranking of first, second or third in the first three classifications which fits the above parameters for the brokerage firm you are using (no commission or very low commission, maximum $25, automatically reinvest dividends) and buy it.

NoLoad Fund*X has 4 basic classifications: *Class 1, Most Speculative; Class 2, Speculative; Class 3, Higher Quality; Class 4, Total Return Funds.* I choose *only* from the first three categories for the greatest return. It doesn't make any difference which category you might wish to choose, but you want the best performing funds in that category. How anyone can classify one mutual fund more speculative than another I don't know. I have always failed to understand how these financial experts rate funds. Some are just *Speculative*, others *Very Speculative*, then there are the *Higher Quality Funds* (does that mean the others are low quality?); maybe some should be called *Retrograde* and others *Gamblers Funds*. To me, the most speculative is the one that *doesn't* perform. Again, this is part of the Wall Street mystique on how to confuse customers into thinking their way instead of using common sense. Most of these Wall Street 'experts' are financial doctors who are doing major surgery on your wallet.

If, over a period of time, any one the funds you have purchased drops out of the top 15 of the *Fund*X* list in its category, sell it immediately. You may have held it in your portfolio for just weeks or it may have been months. Once in a while you might have one for more than a year. Now choose from the top one or two no load funds in any of the first three categories that *No Load Fund*X* rates to replace it. This is rotation. This is the **up** escalator. This is the fastest car on the track, the fastest horse in the race. You are not stalled between floors. You don't want to be riding that horse in the back of the pack because you know what you will be staring at. This is important to attain the greatest return.

Many brokerage companies regularly publish a list of the top performing funds that you may obtain from them at no charge. For example, *Charles Schwab & Co.* will give you the top performers in all categories, broken down by two time periods — best performers for the last 3 months and the last year. Don't go any further back than one year. Three and five year performances are nonsense and don't mean anything to your bottom line. Ten years is really stupid! Ever hear this one: "What have you done for me lately?" From such a list you will probably want to make a comparison between the best for the last year and last 3 months. The mutual funds with the average of the highest 2 numbers will be the best buy. This will require effort and time on your part, but not too much. If you are as lazy as I am, you won't want to do it. Let someone else to do the grunt work. Besides, I like the smoothing effect that *Fund*X* uses by averaging four periods of time. I'm willing to pay the other guy as I have better things to do (like going fishing). By the way, I don't recommend *Schwab* any more because they require you to hold the fund for a minimum of 180 days or they will charge you a large commission. Mr. Schwab has sold out to the poor performers.

When switching from one fund to another, if there is a toss up between two funds I will always pick the one that has the best three-month performance. This is an indication that the fund is currently in stocks that are appreciating faster.

In publications you will see advertisements for many different funds. Figures don't lie but liars can figure, so don't take the numbers at face value until you check them carefully. Look at the ad that appeared in the January 9, 1998 edition of *Investor's Business Daily* for *Lexington Troika Dialog Russia Fund*. Turn the page to see if the numbers in the ad are true; however, the fact remains you would have less money now than you started with a year before. Few people will take the time to compute the value of their funds every day, once a week or even once a month. You can see this clearly on the chart of LETRX. The ad appeared 3 months *after* the time the fund made its contract high. This is one good reason you should make arrangements to have access to the Internet, which you can do at your local library.

DILBERT by Scott Adams

DILBERT reprinted by permission of United Feature Syndicate, Inc.

On May 1, 1997 you plunked down your hard earned $10,000 and bought 609.76 shares at $16.40 of Lexington Russia Fund. Wonderful! Because shortly thereafter it started to go up like a rocket. At the high your "investment" was worth about 150% of what you paid for it. About $25.00 per share (609.76 X $25 = $15,244). That fund manager is really one smart guy!

Unfortunately, it started to go down, but you know the market fluctuates so don't worry, "It will come back". Right?

And you did get some Short Term and Medium Term Capital Gains distributions worth $1.29 per share that you reinvested so you now have 649 shares. However, the price on May 6, 1998, *one year later*, is $14.71. Let's multiply this by 649 to see what your account is worth. No, that can't be right! $9,546. You can't believe it. You have **less** money now than you did a year ago! Maybe I better hold on until it comes back. Where is it today? Go look.

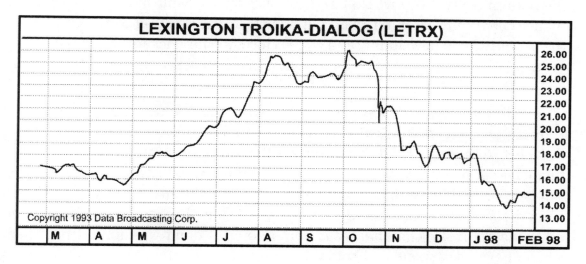

Again, let me repeat what I said above. If you don't want to take time to choose the best funds you could buy the *Vanguard Index 500* (VFINX) mutual fund or some very similar index fund.

Just follow it with your market-timing indicator. However, I know you will do much better staying with the top funds following *NoLoad Fund*X* or some other method of always being with the top performers. Why stay with the average when you can invest in a fund that outperforms the average. Right? Those few extra percentage points make a huge difference over time.

It is not to be implied that you will make big money every month, but it will be rare to *ever* have a losing year. You will never be hoping and praying to get out "even". If the market is in a major correction, whether it is for 3 months or 3 years, you will be out of the equities market and your capital will be safely protected in a money market mutual fund. Don't ride that down escalator!

And you ladies with the blue hair and you old geezers with hair growing out of your ears (like me), don't listen to that stupid broker who wants you to be invested in nice, safe bonds. What you want is a nice, safe return on your money — lots of it! You won't get it in bonds unless it happens when a bond fund finds it way to the top of the performer list; they do, once in a while. This simple method is for anyone of any age. Yes, anyone with two brain cells to rub together can do it. It will take less than one hour per month.

There have been three bear markets since 1970: 1973-74, 1987 and 1990. If you had bought mutual funds in 1969 and waited through the bear market to the bottom of 1974 you would have lost over 45% of your money. It took more than *10 years* in real purchasing power because of inflation to recoup this for the people who believe in Buy and Hold. That's too far back for the "boomers" to remember. They didn't have any money in the market in the 70's. They're gonna getcha next time!

In a bear market you will see funds such as Rydex Ursa (RYURX) and Prudent Bear Fund (BEARX) coming to the top in *NoLoad Fund*X* (they don't list them in the first 3 NoLoad Fund*X categories) and being mentioned in the financial pages. This will occur when you are on a 'sell' signal from *Maverick Advisor, Pitbull Crash Index* or your own generated signal when your cash will be in the money market account. You may now buy these funds, as *they will go up while the rest of the market is going down*. I don't wait long; I buy them when I have a sell signal and hold them until I have another buy signal. This is a way for mutual fund investors to *make money in a down market*. If you are not familiar with bear markets, I suggest investing no more than 50% of your portfolio in these bear funds until you become comfortable with the down (short) side of the market. It moves much faster. Try it. You'll like it.

These next two charts will show you exactly how the bear mutual funds work. Notice the *Vanguard Index 500* and its mirror chart the *Rydex Ursa*. They always move exactly opposite of each other. When the bull market is over and you wish to continue to make money, you have this choice.

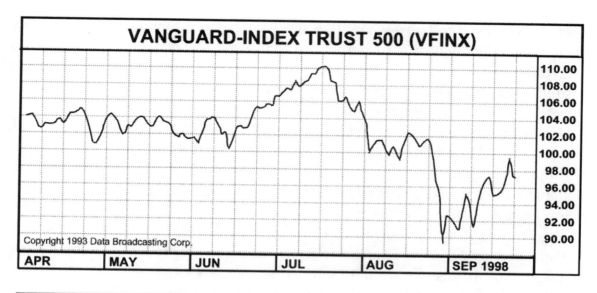

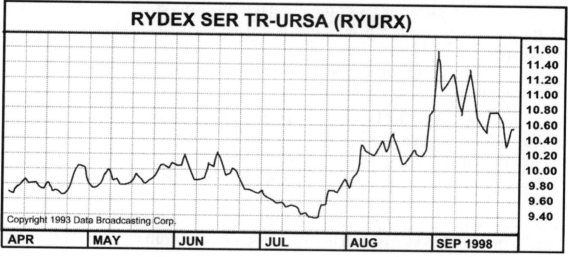

Let me caution you about *NoLoad Fund*X*. They maintain you should be in the market at all times. **Wrong**.

See the *Buy and Hold* exhibit using their numbers on how much you could have *lost* during the brief 1987 break. You will need to study this with a pencil and paper and do some figuring to get the full impact and significance of the table. Then go to the library and look up what your funds did during these same time periods, or you can call the fund's 800 number and get the prices for those specific days. Calculate how much more money you would have had if you had been out of the market during that big break.

You need to know where they are coming from to understand why they say this. *DAL Investment Company* which owns *NoLoad Fund*X* also has a large money management firm with which they are affiliated. They could not suddenly unload several hundred million dollars worth of stock in a day without causing some pretty horrendous results to many issues. But you can! They will also infer that you can't 'time the market'. **Wrong again.** *Fabian's Maverick Advisor* has been doing it for 20 years. You can do it yourself with something as simple as keeping a moving average with the *S&P500 Index* as the buy and sell signal indicator. Investor's Business Daily prints the *S&P* with a 200 day moving average in the chart in each issue. Again I suggest you have a secondary investment indicator index which could be as simple as using the *Dow Jones 65 Composite* or the *Value Line Index* or the *Pitbull Crash Index* with a similar 200 day moving average. When both lines cross you have either a buy or sell.

Another great fallacy of the mutual fund gurus is "expense ratios". They tell you not to invest in any fund that has expenses over 1 ½%. Who cares what the expense ratio is if that fund makes 40% or 50% or 60% or more annually. The same for 12b-1 expenses. Who cares? Show me the bottom line. That's all that counts. Basic rule: Follow the money!

Definitions: **Bull market:** When *Maverick Advisor* or your own indicator has a 'Buy' signal. **Bear market:** When *Maverick Advisor* or your own indicator has a 'Sell' signal. Whatever you do, *don't* listen to brokers or those so-called radio, television and newsletter 'experts' like Bob Brinker, Jay Shabacker, William Rukeyser (my apologies, gentlemen, nothing personal), etc., who say you need a "balanced portfolio" with so much in growth funds and so much in bond funds, so much in cash. They say stick with it for the "long term". *Never.* This is not the way to make 30, 40 or 50% on your money.

The 'talking heads' know all about the market — more than I do, but not anywhere near enough about how to make money. They speak in 'market gobbledegook' language. I marvel at their stupidity because it must be stupidity or they are lying to you. Definitely skip *Wall Street Week* on television; it will do nothing but confuse you. Check their records — you can do better on your own by following the advice in this book. Don't bother to subscribe to those money and financial magazines. (See, I'm already saving you money.) They really don't understand what is going on. If they did, they could not tell you because all their advertisers would leave them. Ask instead what the editors for these magazines are making in their personal portfolios? See if they believe their own propaganda. Most of them couldn't trade their way out of a wet paper bag.

With plain old ordinary common sense you will make more money than those Wall Street 'experts'. *Become a follower,* following the market signals. Do not try to predict the direction of the market or when it will turn up or down. I don't and I make more return on my money than 98% of all the 'experts'.

We recently passed the "10-year-mark" for bragging rights on how well the experts have done with the money they have managed. That was the 1987 crash. The mavens will no longer have to factor in the losses they took, and will be showing you how wonderfully they have done for the past 10 years; some of the results will be rather spectacular. Hey, don't forget they let *you* take all those losses in 1987 and did *not* get you out ahead of that huge break. If you ask about it, you will get some song and dance that has no bearing on the facts. Besides, 10-year studies are meaningless if you want to average 30%, 40% and 50% annually.

Oh yes, one more thing about your mutual funds. When you purchase through any broker or fund family, they will send you a prospectus. Don't read it. Throw it away; it is meaningless. The day it was printed much of the information in it was based on year old facts. What good does this do you? This document was designed to placate the securities laws as written by the Securities and Exchange Commission in Washington. Some bright young attorney at the SEC who knows nothing about making money has read it thoroughly several times to see that it has met all the required regulations, but that doesn't mean it will make any sense, nor will it make you any money. The very worst performing mutual fund will have almost the same identical document as the best performing mutual fund, and could have been approved by the same 'Dilbert' in his Washington cubicle. These are worthless. *Only performance counts!* You won't find that in these documents.

You may receive a prospectus about a new fund coming to the market. It may have great hype with a well-known, high-profile manager and specialize in a currently hot industry group. *Don't buy it.* Anything you buy must have at least a *one-year* track record so you can check its real-time performance. There are plenty of other funds to choose from that have proven their mettle in the actual market. You have no idea if the fund manager can outperform the *S&P 500* or be in the top one percent of all mutual funds. Pass.

The incredibly simple method I have just outlined for you will outperform anything any broker will ever tell you and you can do it yourself without any help from anyone. I keep saying it is easy and safe. Well, there is one hard part. You have to have the discipline to occasionally pick up the phone on the day of the signal to tell the broker to "buy" or "sell". It takes action on your part. You can't be a wimp. You must act when the signal is given. If you can't or won't act yourself, then hire a fee-based financial manager to act by the rules laid out here when a signal is given. Authorize him to follow this method and make the calls for you to your brokerage company. Pay for the subscriptions to these services. (Actually he should be paying you because he can't do that well himself.) Get a signed letter from him that he will follow this program exactly. You might want a second letter from his boss if it is a large organization. He must inform you of his actions. Be sure you check to see he is doing it.

For those of you with 401K's and self-directed pension plans where you are limited to changes within a family of funds, here is what you can do. You will need the *Maverick Advisor* service, *Pitbull* or your own market timing signal, and I recommend at least a 6 month trial of *NoLoad Fund*X* just to get a feel of how their system works. Most companies you work for will allow you to make switches whenever you wish at no commission charge. Even if there is a charge, make the switch. It is to your benefit. You must review monthly all the funds your company allows in order to keep track of their performance. Once you get the hang of charts you will be able to see the best ones at a glance. You might also want to do the work of computing the percentage increase (or decrease) of each fund by month, quarter, 6 month and annually. Add these four percentage numbers then divide by 4. You can do it yourself if you have the time. I don't.

The easiest way to keep track of your 401K portfolio *once a month* is on the Internet. If you don't have a computer at home or Internet access you might try your local library; they probably have both. There are many places where you can rent computer time such as *Kinko's*. Also there are some nice computer coffeehouses that rent computers *On Line*. On the Internet, go to one of the many free sites. I like *CBS MarketWatch* best at:

http://www.marketwatch.com/data/charts/achart.htx

...or to the website of your brokerage firm if they have a chart service.

I have seen many charts from various brokers and there are some that just are very poor. These were obviously created by someone who does not know how to read or understand charts. Type in the symbols for all the different mutual funds in the group to which you are allowed to switch. Print out a hard copy of each one to make a visual comparison. Most of the time it will be pretty obvious which fund is performing best. I like the ones with an **up** angle of at least 30 to 45 degrees. There will always be a money market fund in which to deposit your cash when you get the sell signal from *Maverick Advisor, Pitbull* or the indicator you might choose to calculate yourself.

There are many locations on the Internet that will give free mutual fund information. You will need the fund symbol such as FSFSX for *Invesco Strategic Financial Fund*. Look it up or call the fund itself (they all have a toll free numbers, but most don't provide charts). Follow the directions on your monitor; you will be able to retrieve a picture (chart) of each of the funds that you are allowed to trade. Print all these so you can study them to make comparisons. Usually you can see at a glance which ones are moving up and which ones are going sideways or down. It should be rather obvious where you should have your money. Rotate. *Switch* to the one having the greatest percentage gain. You may want to diversify your money into several if you have a choice among 10 or more funds. You could be in 2 or 3 or 4 of the best. It is doubtful you will be making very many switches, as groups tend to stay in a trend for long periods of time — at least several months, sometimes over a year.

Almost without exception you will read articles from mutual fund managers and brokerage companies about the folly of trading mutual funds. When you are riding in a horserace you don't care what the name of the horse is as long as it is the fastest. The same for mutual funds you don't care what the name of the fund is as long as it is out-performing all the others. They like to call it "hot money" to make it sound nasty. Call it what you will, but if you don't keep your hard-earned money with the best performing funds you can call it "stupid money". Let me make it clear that I am not saying you will be switching from one fund to another every month. In 1998 I had a total of eleven offsets. The only time you will buy a new fund will be when one of the funds you own drops below 15th place in the *Fund*X* schedule (or whatever method you are using to track the top performing funds). You sell it, thereby having money to buy into one of the current top performing funds or when you sell everything to put all your money into a money market account.

Fund managers have an ulterior motive to keep you with their fund. They want to hold on to your money as long as possible because they get paid by the *amount* of money they have under management, *not* on performance. See why they say to stay with one fund forever, *even if it goes down*. Whatever smoke and mirrors reason they give you, don't accept it. Most of the newsletter writers, analysts, newspaper and magazine reporters have been brainwashed into believing this garbage. Think for yourself; don't let them think for you.

Hopefully some day the federal government may modify the Social Security program so you can have a special self-directed investment account. What all the rules and regulations will be I can't begin to think of as the political mind is much too devious for me. If you are allowed to direct your money to the mutual funds of your choice and will follow the simple method above you will be able to retire (if they let you) long before any of your peers. You definitely don't want any government committee picking stocks for you. Keep control.

Reprinted with permission

In case you don't know it there is no Social Security "trust fund". The money they take out of your paycheck every week goes into the General Fund;

they spend it on anything they want.

I won't get on my Social Security soapbox because it is not important what I think about this. You should take an active stand that will allow you to control your own money investments. You worked for the money! Payments you are making into Social Security are *your* money even though the politicians spend it like it was theirs. If we can just siphon some of it off from that great government Ponzi scheme, how lovely that would be.

If you don't have an IRA you should. It allows taking advantage of huge tax savings. Currently you are allowed to put in $2,000 and all dividends and capital gains are shielded from current taxes. Discuss this with your accountant.

You are easily smart enough to take advantage of these tax savings. When you open an IRA with one of the major discount brokerage houses and you put in $166.67 every month — $2,000 annually — here is what can happen:

Ask yourself this question. Is it worth the effort for me to put in one hour each month for this kind of return? These are *not* pie-in-the-sky numbers. You can do it, but *you* must be disciplined enough to do it consistently every month.

Let's switch the question around. How soon do I want to be able to quit

MONTHLY	TIME	INTEREST	ACCUMULATION*
$166.67	20 year	10 %	$ 162,561
$166.67	20 year	15%	$ 249,544
$166.67	20 year	20%	$ 518,275
$166.67	20 year	25%	$1,119,874
$166.67	20 year	30%	$2,491,636
$166.67	20 year	40%	$5,979,036

*Taxes not computed

my job, get away from my boss, travel and live off the income from my investments? Do you want to wait until you are 65 or 70? You probably don't need to go the full 20 years for that. The $166.67/month at 30% could turn into more than $300,000 in 15 years. With $300,000 in your account you would have an approximate annual income of $90,000 a year projecting a 30% return, only $60,000 per year at 20%. Can you make it on that?

These next two paragraphs are for you dummies who call yourself fund

DILBERT by Scott Adams

DILBERT reprinted by permission of United Feature Syndicate, Inc.

managers and can't beat the *S&P500*. It is easy to do, but you will have to do some intelligent work. Not much...less than the nonsense you are doing now. As you know, there are 500 stocks composing this index. In a bull market, among the 500 issues, probably only 100 are worth owning — probably less. Just go through all 500 stocks and simply look at the chart for each one. Print out a daily and weekly bar chart for each stock. Forget that BS about "research". Just make a comparison and maybe use a simple oscillator like MACD or stochastics for timing and ROC (rate of change in price). For you folks who don't know what these technical indicators are, it really doesn't make any difference. If the price is going down or sideways, either don't buy it or sell it. Doing this you will beat the index performance because the *Index Funds* have positions in all 500 stocks. Why would you want to be invested in the dogs? The truth is you fund managers have been good students, but badly taught. You should do this every month. Weekly is better. Oh yes, and when one of the stocks gets weak enough to sell, take the proceeds and put the cash into the strongest stock, not a new one. If you can't beat the *S&P500 Index* with this simple method you are even dumber than I think you are.

If you have any computer smarts you could write a short program which would find the strongest stocks. I would keep culling the weak ones until I had only 50 or 60 stocks for my portfolio. When you get to your magic number of issues sell out any non-performing stock. Then you can then go into the other 450 to find a new stock. I know. This is way too simple for you Wall Street folks who like to make things complicated.

Oh well, I tried.

Actually, the best of both worlds is to have a discount broker — low commissions and no advice. Then you trade your own system. In this book you are going to find several simple methods which don't require much time or effort don't require a computer, don't require mathematical equations, don't require 'research' and don't require 'advice' from a know-nothing broker, but will make you all the money you need sooner than you think. Then you can tell your boss to get lost. I'm *not* an advocate of full-time trading because having a regular job does keep you off the street and gives you something else to think about other than the markets. Besides, you would become pretty boring after awhile and lose your friends. You won't have anything to talk about in which they are also interested

If you have read this far you either love me or hate me. My critics say I am too simplistic and I say they are too complicated. The only yardstick for comparison is who makes more money. I'll challenge any one of them. You get too, too much information and most of it you don't need. It is nonsense propaganda designed to confuse the little investor. The simpler the plan the better it works. KISS me.

I am not a prognosticator (sure sounds like a dirty word). I don't try to predict the future. I am a follower; following the currently smartest fund managers, riding their coattails to my bank. You don't have to be smart when using this simple method, just smart enough to know that you can't do as well trying to pick individual stocks yourself.

Imagine if all the mutual fund owners did what I have outlined here. There would be a lot of mutual fund managers out looking for a job; maybe they are qualified as janitors or school bus drivers or hamburger flippers, but certainly not money managers.

For as long as I can remember, the great majority of investors have been hornswoggled, boondoggled, bamboozled, BS'd, dumped on, lied to, conned, mesmerized, deceived, double-dealt, smooth-talked, equivocated, fibbed to, humbugged, perplexed, bewildered, shafted, shammed, beguiled, mystified, defrauded, and a few more you can name. Brokers wave hundreds of sheets of slick, colored paper they call "research" across your eyes until you believe it means something. It doesn't. Smoke and mirrors. Forget research. Forget reports. Forget all that nonsense and remember only one thing:

PERFORMANCE! PERFORMANCE! PERFORMANCE!

It is *your* money! Do not listen to the hype of a bunch of professional losers — that's any fund manager who can't beat the *S&P500*. The one basic rule you absolutely MUST follow: If your fund can't beat the *S&P 500 Index*, sell it and find one that does. Stay with the top performers, the top 1% of all funds. You won't be making switches very often. If you have 5 funds I doubt it will be 5 times a year because once you are in a good performer it will usually continue to be on top of the heap for quite a while.

Let me summarize:

1. **You will own mutual finds when the market is going up**
   based on the "BUY" signal from *Fabian's Maverick Advisor*, *Pitbull Crash Index* or your own market timing method.

2. **You will be in cash when the market is going down**
   based on the "SELL" signal from *Fabian's Maverick Advisor*, *Pitbull* or your own market timing method.

3. **You will know which funds are the best to own**
   when the market is going up

4. **You will choose from the ratings of the best performing**
   mutual funds shown in *NoLoad Fund*X*.

Follow the signals as they are generated and you will maximize income and protect your capital. Check my web site at **www.mutualfundmagic.com** for additional money-making reference material as it becomes available. You will have profits and peace of mind. And remember...

IF IT DOESN'T GO UP, DON'T BUY IT!

Stocks

Before we go any further, you may be asking yourself if this guy (me) knows what he is talking about? How did he get so smart to write a book like this? It didn't happen overnight.

In 1960 I sued the guy I was working for because he fired me; it was the only job I ever had where I worked for a salary. After that I either worked on straight commission or owned or controlled the company. That is one of only two lawsuits I have ever filed because I don't believe in suing people unless I have really been screwed. Well, to make a long story short, I won. He had to pay me $2400 of which my attorney took $800. That left me with the huge amount of $1600.

A stockbroker acquaintance offered to help me 'invest' it so I could make some money. Of course, that sounded great so I opened an account with his brokerage company. I was inundated with the usual stuff brokerage firms send out. You know, pink sheets, green sheets, yellow sheets, annual reports, interim reports, prospectuses, etc., etc. Let's just call it what it really is — garbage. It is not even good for toilet paper. He was your typical "churner" and "burner". That's a broker who gives you lots of trading action and burns through your money. He did manage to keep me even with his commissions. When you think about it that is better than what most brokers do. After several months of excitement with lots of action, but no profits, I was at his office on LaSalle Street (like Wall Street, but in Chicago) where he showed me his stock charts. Whammo! It was a blaze of understanding. Immediately I could see the orderliness of the price patterns. I said, "This is the way to trade". That was the start of my technical analysis education.

I bought some graph paper and started to make my own charts. Back in the early 60's there were very few chart services. They were expensive and I didn't have much money. Within a few months I was keeping 40 daily bar charts of various stocks and 200 weeklies. I did this for years. Living close to the University of Chicago Library I spent hours reading as much as I could find on technical analysis — but there wasn't much then. *(You are not going to have to learn any of this.)*

One of the old books I found in the reserve stacks was called *Tape Reading* by Rollo Tape, obviously a pseudonym. Richard Wyckoff, one of the first technical analysts, wrote it. He was good enough to die rich in the 1930's. His work is still taught today under various names and I consider it to be one of the key foundations of technical analysis. Some time later I met and became good friends with Mr. Ellis Luke who knew and worked with the Wyckoff material. He taught me a lot more than just the Wyckoff analysis.

Mr. Wyckoff made a clear association between price and volume. Whichever way the volume increases, up or down, points the direction of the stock or commodity price. It took me several days to transcribe his book (we didn't have copiers back then). His analysis worked then and it still works now. The way I have outlined for you is much easier.

More about my "expensive education" later.

INVESTOR OR SPECULATOR?

Most investors say, "I'm in for the long term so I really don't watch the market. My broker (money market manager, banker, attorney, brother-in-law, etc.) takes care of everything for me, so I don't have to worry". You better worry or you are headed for the cleaners. It is *your money* and no one has more interest in it than you do! Your broker doesn't like to call you with bad news so he just doesn't call you until it is too late. Then he will give you that old lame one, "Maybe we ought to hold on to this for a while longer and I'm sure it will come back". And pigs can fly! Often it takes years before a mutual fund or stock works its way back up to where it was at the old highs. The average is *10 years*. You don't have to be an 'expert' to avoid these down markets. Always remember you are *not* an "investor", *you are a speculator whether you like it or not*. Only the time frame is different. You can't rely on someone else to play with your money. Anytime YOU are not in complete control of your money you are speculating.

One of Woody Allen's movie characters was asked what he did for a living and said he was a financial manager. "What do you do?" "I manage people's money until it is all gone." More truth than fiction.

by Charles Petersen

Let me ask you: If you owned a business (an employment agency, a manufacturing or service company, a shoe store, a gas station), wouldn't you want to see the bottom line weekly or monthly? Are sales rising or falling? How are you doing compared to your competition? Is your return on investment doing what other businesses of this type are yielding? Are you making any money? You can't run any business hands off because someone else's hands are going to be in your pocket. It won't work. That guy who is managing your money wants to be paid and it is almost always with commissions, not performance. No broker will work on a percentage of profits and deep discount commissions because the industry has made regulations against his being allowed to do this.

Money talks and it doesn't speak more loudly than in Washington where they make the laws which govern what *you* can and cannot do with *your* money. Guess who sponsored and lobbied for this legislation?

Your so called 'money manager' should be paid on performance only. Most money managers charge a fee based on the size of your portfolio. Is that a rip-off, or what? He doesn't even have to make you a penny, and he gets to skim off the top every year. You need your head examined to fall for this one.

In my opinion, you should never let your 'financial manager' charge you a fee based on the value of your portfolio. Let's say he does an average job and your return is 12%. Is it really 12%? Take out his 2% to 3 % (plus those hidden "fees"), adjust for inflation, then pay your taxes (you put in this figure) and see if you have 3 or 4% left as your real profit. Probably not. Get another 'manager' — *yourself* — and you will do a better job with higher returns.

Now I'm going to hit you in the head with a 2X4 to see if I can get your attention. Wham! If you are not willing to invest one hour per month reviewing your investments and making your own decisions, then you deserve to lose money or get a miserable return on your investments. Wham! How many times do I have to whack you? Wham! Bang! Crunch! You got it? Then *do* it!

When you have a mutual fund, stock, or commodity and it is going against you (meaning you are losing your shirt, pants, underwear and having stomach pains to boot) and you call your broker he might say, "Hey, this is great. Now, you can buy many more shares. We can *dollar-cost average*," he says proudly, "and when it starts going up again you will make a fortune". Please notice he said 'we', but it's *your* money going down the drain. Guess who thought up this brutally stupid idea. Some broker! He got his customer into 500 shares of *Broken Mouse Trap* (symbol: NUTS) at $50/share and it has dropped to $20. "You know, Mr. Mushroom, if you buy 500 more shares you will have an average price of $35. Isn't that great?"

This scenario is called *Dumb and Dumber*. The broker's advice is dumb and the customer is even dumber. Averaging down is a guaranteed loser. The brokerage house (definition: "bookie"), the broker (definition: "runner"), the professional investment adviser (definition: "tout"), the financial magazines (the "Green Sheet") — none of them want you to think they don't know what they are doing so they came up with this cockamamie idea. Don't fall for it. There is only one way to dollar cost average (if you want to) and that is *after* you have profit in that first purchase. You average **up**, not down. Here is the skinny of it.

1. When any broker, banker, financial planner, analyst (that's pronounced with a broad 'a'), etc. recommends a stock, bond, call, put, anything (!) — your first question to him should be, "If I buy it here, *where do I sell* it? " This will usually stop him in his tracks. After an appropriate moment of silence he will start talking about how much profit you will make when you "take the long term view". No! No! No! That is not what you want to hear. Your *first* concern is, "How much can I lose? Where do I get out if this is the top of the move? Where do I put in an open stop loss?" Be sure you get a written confirmation of the stop-loss order. (We will discuss "stops" later.)

2. *Never add to a losing position*. Nine out of ten times the stock or commodity will rally back and you will be able to get out even (if you can wait long enough). One time out of ten you will go broke. When dollar cost averaging in a winning position, 9 out of 10 times the stock or commodity will fall back and you will get out even (usually sooner than you want to). One time out of ten you will make a small fortune. Buying new contract highs (that's a higher price than the stock has ever been in the past) is one of the safest and most profitable ways of trading because there is no one trying to 'get out even' on stock he bought several years ago.

You don't want to get out 'even', you want to get out wealthy.

LONG TERM DOUBLE TOP

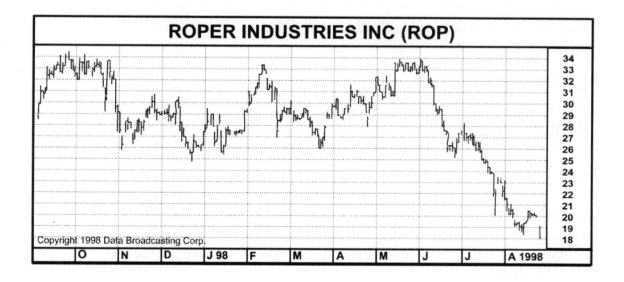

When I say, "If it doesn't go up, don't buy it" I mean exactly that. If you must buy individual issues (and I don't recommend this for the small investor) then take a long look at a chart of the stock going back for 5 years. On the Internet you can download 1-year, 3- year and 5-year bar charts from **www.cbsmarketwatch.com**. Study all three charts carefully. First, the stock should be making new contract high prices over the previous five years. The angle of upward movement should be 30 to 45 degrees on the *weekly* chart. Any idiot can buy. It takes intelligence to know when to sell. Read the section on "STOPS" which follows. You will find that once a trend starts it will last a long time.

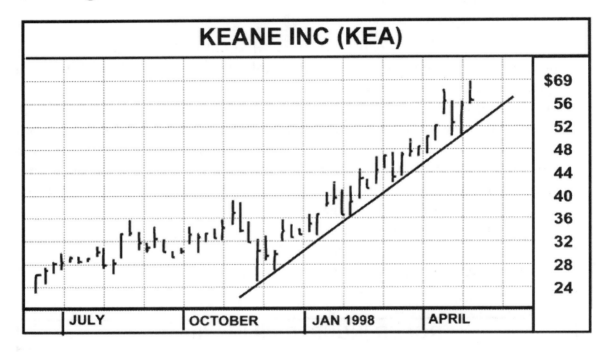

Don't trade "thin" issues — stocks that trade less than 30,000 shares per day can be dangerous. If there is a sudden downdraft, there will not be enough buy orders under the market to give you a decent "fill" (execution at the price you want) when your stop is hit. This doesn't apply to mutual funds.

There is something called the "time value of money". It could be months, sometimes years before the stock rallies back to where you bought it so you can get out 'even'. When a stock or mutual fund drops 50% it means it must go up 100% before you can get out 'even'. Well, you're not 'even'. What could you have earned with that same money even if you had it invested at only 5% in T-Bills? And in commodities and options you don't have the time to wait; you must get out or take delivery and you don't want that. (You may have heard the story about the poor dummy who had a carload of frozen pork bellies dumped on his front lawn. It isn't true and never will be, but they keep telling it.) The stock trader can sit fat, dumb and happy and say, "I'll wait for it to come back". He has his head in a dark place.

Never let a profitable trade go to a loss. Once you have a profit in a stock or commodity trade *bring your stop up to break even as soon as you can.* You can sleep better at night and you don't have to read the stock section every morning (but you probably will anyway).

STOPS

The first formal training I took back in the 60s was with an old trader from Detroit named Bert Larson. Bert has probably long since gone to Stock Heaven where he never has a down tic or a losing trade on his positions. I paid $250 for the 6 weeks of classes which was pretty pricey by the day's standard, but was worth it. That workbook on technical analysis (if only I could ever find it, but I gave away my total library when my wife Carolyn and I bought a 41 foot world-class ketch — that's a 2-masted sailboat for you folks in Oklahoma — and we took off for 2 years) would be applicable today. He did an excellent job of pounding into my head that you should always trade with stops. Fortunately I learned it then, but it took many years for me to learn other things. I went broke twice trading commodities before I got smart enough to keep my money. All part of my expensive trading education.

This is the most important rule for any trader or investor or whatever you want to call yourself. Always *place an open stop (GTC means 'good until cancelled') when you put on the trade.* "Stops make you money!" I've said that 10,000 times if I've said it once. Most people won't do it. You know why? Their ego gets in the way of common sense. Everyone thinks his trade will be profitable and he is counting the dollars and how he is going to spend them. He never thinks his trade can go south in a hurry. He's standing there with his finger up his nose or some other warm place wondering what went wrong. (You know that only happens to other people, never to you.) He keeps telling himself, " I know it will come back and then I'll sell". Ho boy!

"I've tried putting in stops, but those floor traders go after my stop and I always lose money". How many times have I heard that one from customers. Folks, that's not true. You did not have your stop in a logical spot. Better yet, go back and look at where you were stopped out and see if it ever made a new high or it started going down. The latter is more likely. Go ahead. Check it!

Another one of the stupid things people do when trading stocks is to sell the trade that is profitable and hang on to the trade that is in the dumpers waiting for it to come back. Look at your own portfolio. See if there aren't some stocks and mutual funds that you have had for a long time and are now less than you paid for them. Why are they still there? Why haven't you cleaned house? Get rid of those dogs and put that money to work in a potentially profitable trade. Foolish consistency is the hobgoblin of little minds. You must start thinking differently if you are going to make big money regularly.

During the Great Depression of the nineteen thirties, *Filene's* (a department store in Boston) came up with a plan to get rid of their slow moving merchandise. If the piece of clothing had not sold during the "season", the store then started marking it down 10% every week until someone bought it. They were able to get rid of their "dogs" even if it meant taking a substantial loss and were able to buy new merchandise that could make them a profit. The Filene Plan is still used today and maybe you should think about applying a similar modified plan to your portfolio.

Let's look at one of the worst things that can happen when you own a stock and your open stop (an open stop is placed with your broker and is put in daily by the brokerage house until you cancel it) is not only hit, but also completely demolished. Look at the *Silicon Graphics* (SGI) chart and suppose

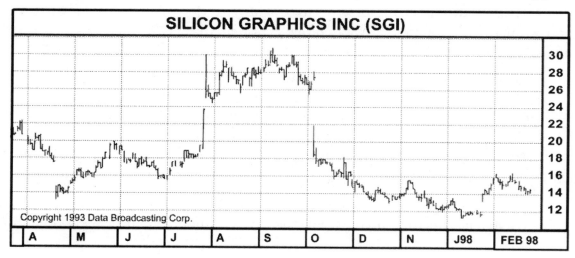

you owned 1,000 shares for which you paid $28 a share — $28,000. If you had been trailing a $2.80 stop (10%) the market opened at $21 one day in October 1997 with a gap down (that's where there is no trading at any price) and your stop was executed at $20. Your $8,000 is down the drain. That takes your breath away! Now let's suppose you didn't have that stop and you decided to wait for it to "come back and then I'll get out". Heard that story before? Well, by February 1998 you are still waiting. Unfortunately your loss has grown to $14,000, $15,000 or $16,000 plus a terrible pain in your mid-section each time you look at the quote in the paper. Your stop would have had you out and $8,000 *ahead*. I will repeat, "STOPS MAKE YOU MONEY!"

Remember a few years ago when every broker in the world was recommending Boston Chicken (BOST)? Did he ever call you to tell you to sell? Or get short? Did he even recommend a stop? See how much money your 10% stop would have saved you. Again, "STOPS MAKE YOU MONEY!" I'm yelling. I'm screaming!

Years ago I heard how they used to catch monkeys in Africa. The hunters would take a coconut shell which was attached to a strong thin rope, make a hole in it just the size of a monkey's empty outstretched hand. The rope was tied to a stake that was pounded firmly into the ground. In the coconut were berries and nuts that the monkeys liked very much. The monkeys would smell the aroma of the fruit and nuts, put their hands into the coconut and make a fist around the goodies. When they tried to withdraw their full fist it would not come out of the hole even when they saw the hunter coming for them. They would not let go of their prize even if it meant capture and imprisonment. *That is the same as holding onto a losing position* in commodities, stocks, mutual funds or anything. A stop will get you out automatically and you won't have to think about it.

The experienced trader — the true professional — thinks first about the risk of the trade before he thinks about how much he is going to make. He wants to have ammunition left for another target in case he misses this one. That is why they make repeating rifles and six shooters. I know I am happy, if at the end of my fiscal year, I have had 50% winners in my stock and option trading. During 1998 I had eleven mutual fund offsets, all profitable. People talk about "money management" all the time and somehow manage to disguise it when it really should be called "risk management". *Your goal is to maximize profits and minimize risk in any area in which you choose to invest.*

You have a finite amount of money to play with. Does 'play with' offend you? It shouldn't because, call it what you wish, that is what you, or your 'conservative' money manager (that oxymoron again) are doing. Over the course of years you will not need very many good (profitable) trades to make yourself a fortune. Finding them is the problem and stops will help you survive to do this. You should divide your money into 10 segments and by this I mean you can put all your money on one stock if you want to, but you must put in that stop-loss order. Using the 10% stop rule means you can make 10 losing trades before you go broke. Hey, it happens, but it also means that you have 10 chances to be right at finding that one huge winner — like Apple Computers when it first came out, or Intel, or _____ (you put your favorite in the blank). If you hadn't put in a stop (and either been stopped out with a small loss or many times a profit), you would be riding a dead horse, or broke. Keep moving your stop up *every* week as it rises and you will have your profit locked in.

It is difficult to have a system in which you are being stopped out several times as all you see are small losses and no big profits, but by remaining with your system you will survive to find the big hitter.

Figure out before you take the position just exactly how much you are willing to risk. 5%, 10%... more? As a general rule I like 10%, but many times my stop is much closer. I am nibbling at the position and will add to it as it starts to go up. It is proving out that my analysis is correct. I like to buy 'breakouts' after a long period of trading in a small price range. For example, if a stock has been trading in a range of $27 to $30 for 6 months or more and suddenly closes over $30 I will buy this new high close. Whatever it is, I place a Good 'Til Canceled (GTC) Stop with my broker *before* I hang up.

Stops make you money! That doesn't sound right does it? Think about this. Without that stop you would hope and pray the market would rally to let you out even. But the position gets worse and worse until you finally can't stand it any longer and have lost everything. If you had a 10% stop you would still have 90% of your money and could find an opportunity for another trade. When you're broke, you are out of the game!

Let me give you a personal example of one trade I made. In May/June of 1996, I bought several positions at an average price of $23 per share in *Black Box* (See BBOX chart) *after* the breakout above $21 and immediately

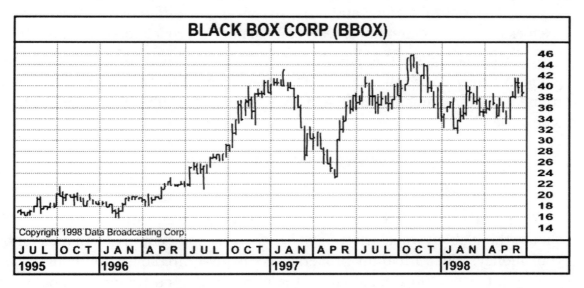

put in my trailing open stop. It moved up nicely and I was stopped out in October at $36 after it hit $40. A 57% cash profit in only 5 months. Then it continued to go up *after* I was stopped out, all the way to $43! Did I feel like a dummy? NO!! I had taken a good profit and went on to find another stock. Then look what happened. It dropped all the way down to $21, which was lower than where I originally bought at $23. Now am I a dummy? And today it has rallied back to where I got out. I don't like this kind of roller coaster ride. Makes me look smart when all I did was put in a stop. You can do this too.

Why do people do dumb things like monkeys? Because they don't want to admit to being wrong. People don't like being wrong about anything. For years I have been saying the reason people trade is to find out what kind of person they are. It is totally psychological. They are not trading to make money. It seems most of them want to find out how much pain they can stand. Players don't like to sit on the sidelines.

There is *one* time I do not advocate the use of stops and that is when you are following the mutual fund program I have laid out here. It applies only to the funds in your timing portfolio. The reason you don't need the stops in this particular instance is because you will sell them *all* when you have a Sell signal from *Maverick Advisor* or when a particular fund drops below fifteenth place in the *NoLoad Fund*X* bulletin.

Poor risk management will not only make you broke but will also break you psychologically. Please — put in those stops. Money management is the key to all successful trading and it doesn't make any difference what you trade — stocks, bonds, commodities, real estate, paintings, collectibles, stamps, etc.

Another quicky thought here. Don't associate with losers. It is contagious. All they do is tell you it can't be done and tell you how they or their friend lost everything playing the market. Stay off the subject with them or get a new friend.

CHOOSING A BROKER

If you want one.

I hate to seem like I'm death on brokers, but there are some things you should think about when selecting one. I was one and I cut my teeth on a lot of your money. When I had my brokerage company I hired over 300 bodies (not brokers). Of the 300 I could count the number of good traders on one hand and have fingers left over. Doesn't build your confidence does it? Brokerage companies do not hire people because they can trade profitably; they hire them because they can open new accounts and generate commissions. They just want your money. Got it?

What I say about brokers applies not only to commodity brokers but ALL brokers — stocks, bonds and options. Anything.

Be careful of any broker who advocates fading the market. "Mr. Mushroom, this stock (bond, mutual fund) has gone down so far that it has to go up from here." See the *Boston Chicken* chart. This is a death wish for your bank account. These people have an ego problem; they think they know more than the market. Believe me, they don't.

SHOE by Jeff MacNelly

Let me tell you about one broker I worked with before I owned my own company. He saved up enough to buy a seat on the Chicago Mercantile Exchange. A big, tall, good-looking guy with an ego bigger than a moose, I knew his trading style and how he used to wipe out his customers with that fading technique. Sure enough. We had a limit up day in the cattle and Ed went in and sold all the bids in the back month. He then tried to muscle the market down by offering even more. You guessed it. They didn't come off limit bid and he didn't have the money. The Exchange confiscated his membership which they sold and he was gone leaving a large debit the house had to eat.

Bottom pickers just have smelly fingers.

If your broker is not giving you the service you feel is commensurate with the commission you are paying (full service/discount) then get another one.

Don't deal with a relative. Do I have to explain this one?

Don't deal with a friend, especially if you live in a small town. Everyone in his office can have access to your account statements and will know what you are doing and you certainly don't want people to know when you pick a real stinker or lose all your money because you failed to put in stops.

If a broker calls you and says he has a "system" for trading and can make money for you, just hang up. He is a liar. If it was such a great system why is he calling you? He would be trading his own account and would not have to bother with nutty customers. Many brokers consider their customers "mooches". Some I have heard referred to as "mushrooms". I wonder why. Could it be because they are kept in the dark and fed horse manure?

If a broker calls and talks service, service, service. Listen. Find out how many years he has been in the business and if he has a personal trading account. Some companies do not allow it. Most do. Brokerage houses will take money from anyone, even their own people. The minimum time in the business should be 5 years, 15 is better. Maybe you can even get him to send you copies of his personal account to see if he does know what he is doing. He might. You could give this guy a trial if you insist on trading, but you really don't want any advice.

Even today I am often solicited by brokers and advisory services that send me great information on how much money they are making for their clients. I send them a letter asking the following:

1. Is this a real-time track record or is it hypothetical? (You can trash it right here if it is hypothetical.)

2. What is the minimum size account I need to take *all* your signals?

3. Assuming all trades were taken for the previous year, what was the starting amount of the account and the amount at the end of the year including commissions?

4. What was the largest single draw down (loss)?

5. What was the largest continuous draw down?

6. Do you use stops?

7. Do you experience slippage on stops?

8. How many winning trades?

9. What was the average profit?

10. How many losing trades.

11. What was the average loss?

12. Do you recommend a particular broker to trade the system?

13. How long have you been using this system?

14. Please send a printout of last year's monthly statements.

More than likely you will not get an answer. They may use the excuse that it is proprietary information. But, if you are satisfied and do sign up with them do it with the proviso, in writing, that they will give the names of 3 of their customers with whom you may speak and who have been trading the method for at least a year. Don't trade the system until you have spoken with those people. Hopefully, they will tell you the truth.

There is one investment advisory service that takes full page ads showing many stocks and how they have appreciated from their buy signal to the top of the move in that stock. Unfortunately, they never tell you where to sell. They don't publish the losers. Anyone foolish enough to buy a service like this had better use stops.

I was soliciting new commodity accounts on the phone and during the conversation I told the man that I had been brought up on a farm. He immediately challenged me with these questions: "What color is a John Deere tractor?" I said, "Green". "What color is a Farmall tractor?" I said, "Red". "What color is a Ford Ferguson?" I said, "Gray". I knew them all as he went down every tractor he could think of. He agreed and said, "You had to be raised on a farm to know that". He did open an account.

The difference between stocks and commodities is like the difference between a Formula One and a kiddy car. That's the reason stock brokers can't trade commodities. Stockbrokers can't drive this Formula One. Stockbrokers are not trained to think for themselves despite what they tell you.

RESEARCH

The big brokerage houses hire research analysts. This is definitely pronounced with a broad 'a'. It's usually some kid out of college who can read. He puts together all the known information with pretty charts the way they taught him in school and makes a nice report. He even talks to the president of the company and this is the last guy you want to interview. Anyone with two brain cells to rub together knows he is not going to tell you anything bad about his company. The kid's college professor forgot to tell him the purpose of a research report was to make money. But the report is pretty.

We used to have a guy who came to our office to write commodity reports that the company offered free in their advertising. "Sure, I can write you a good story about soybeans. Do you want it bullish or bearish?" He didn't care. He had all the "research" and all he had to do was slant the material. He also wrote stock reports.

There are big brokerage houses and huge companies that pay $20,000, $30,000 or more annually for research reports and then don't follow them. They buy the reports for political reasons — they have to show their shareholders that they are getting "the best" information available from big name think tanks in New York, London or Washington. Most of the very top executives know better than to heed the advice of someone who has never been on the firing line.

The right way to do research is to go to that company and get permission to wander around without an escort if they will let you. Very doubtful. (Maybe you will have to do it without permission). Somehow, without a chaperone, you want to talk to the guy on the shipping platform and he should not know who you are. Take off your coat and tie, take a clipboard and tell him you are checking the fire extinguishers. Have some coffee with him. Let him talk. You will find out more in 15 minutes than 3 days in the front office. I heard of one researcher who was smart enough to sit in his car for 3 days outside the company loading platform and count the number of company trucks taking out shipments. He knew approximately what the valuation of each load should be and then extrapolated to get an educated guess as to company sales. It was far off from what he was told by the big brass. With a little more checking he found he was right.

Most research information you can find is already ancient history. If you can get it you can be sure everyone else knows it. If everyone else knows it then all that information is currently reflected in the stock price. Most research is basically worthless.

UPGRADES AND DOWNGRADES

Let me let you prove to yourself how useless these researchers for the big brokerage houses are. On January 14, 1998 *Investor's Business Daily* published the upgrades and downgrades for various stocks. They do this just about every day. On this particular day the research analyst for Paine Webber *upgraded* MBNA (listed on the NYSE, symbol KRB) to "Neutral" from "Unattractive". Don't ask me what that means. This is the kind of mysterious language these people use to keep you confused — their lips move, they make sounds, but they don't say anything intelligible. Your broker will explain it — ha ha! On the *same day* the research maven at Morgan Stanley Dean Witter Discover *downgraded* MBNA to "Outperform" from "Strong buy". Please don't ask me which of these two geniuses is going to be right. For the previous 6 months the stock had traded on a range from 25 to 30 — you'd have watched your investment go nowhere. This is like the chicken sitting on the china egg.

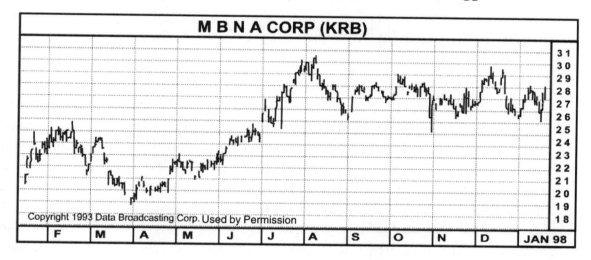

On this very same day a brokerage house — UBS Securities — downgraded Toys R Us (TOY, listed on the NYSE) to "Buy" from "Strong Buy". On the first of December it was trading at 34 (where it had been for months) as a 'strong buy' and on January 14, 1998 it was down to 26. Maybe if it drops another 25% they might tell you to 'hold' or call it 'neutral' or some other nonsensical term.

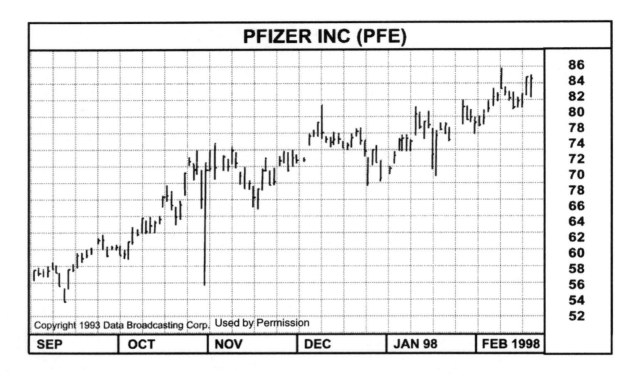

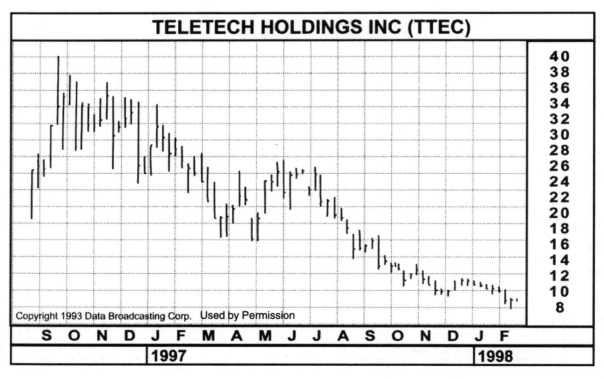

56

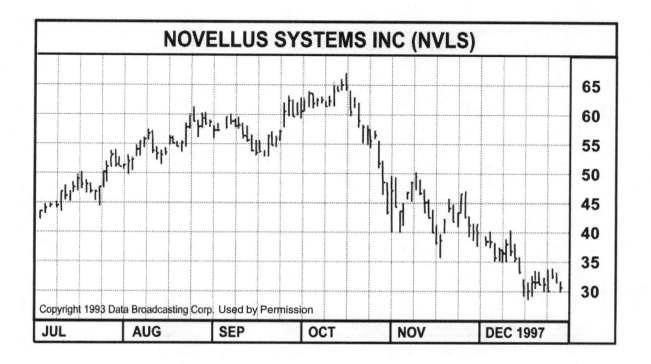

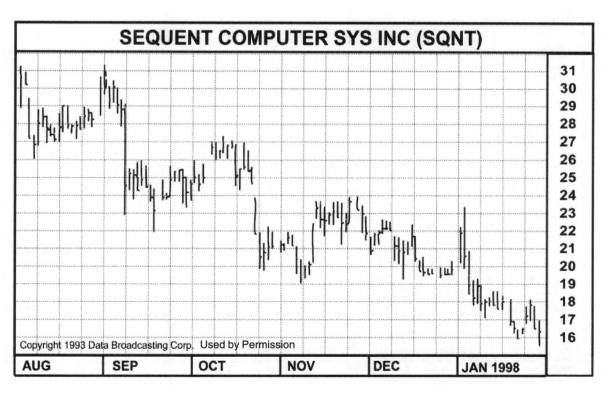

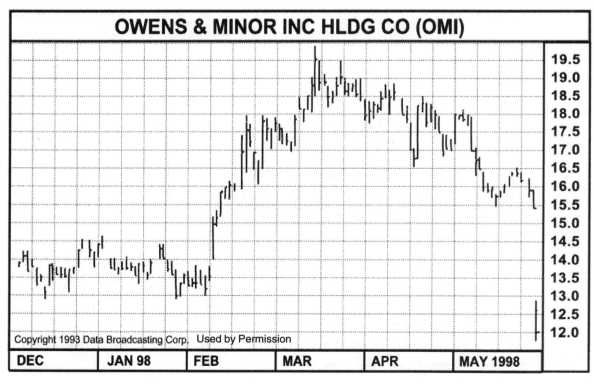

Whatever it's called, it is a losing position. If you had a 10% stop you would have been out with more cash in your pocket or with a different profitable stock position than you would have at this time.

Pfizer (PFE) is a real puzzler. Here is a stock with a nice steady upward move underway, yet Southeast Research Partners on February 11, 1998 downgraded it to "Hold" from "Buy". Why do you tell investors to stop buying a stock that is moving higher and higher and at other times tell them to keep buying a stock that is going lower and lower? Maybe their research knows something that common sense does not. I think I can live without it.

Another research fiasco is Teletech Holdings (TTEC). Raymond James on February 10, 1998 finally downgraded this dog from "Accumulate" to "Neutral". Have you been accumulating this from 38 all the way down to 9? I hope you have more sense than that. Think of how much you could lose by "dollar cost averaging" this puppy.

Look at what Lehman Brothers did with Novellus Systems on December 19, 1997. They downgraded this from "Outperform" to "Neutral". What the heck was it outperforming while it was losing more than 50% of its value?

On January 29, 1998 Merrill Lynch made two recommendations on Sequent Computer Systems (SQNT). Now it is a short term "Neutral" from Accumulate", but they are keeping their long-term recommendation as "Accumulate". Maybe you can keep accumulating this one all the way down to four. Isn't averaging down just great? Yeah, average down right into the poor house.

Please notice I am not playing any favorites. Know this — that all the brokerage houses qualify for equal stupidity. Just a couple more:

CS First Boston and Prudential Securities both downgraded Green Tree Financial (GNT) on January 27, 1998. First Boston to "Hold" from "Buy" and Prudential to "Neutral" from "Buy". There is no bottom in either one of these charts. I hope you didn't own any.

One more for the road: Salomon Smith Barney on May 28, 1998 downgraded Owens & Minor (OMI) from "Buy" to "Outperform"(?). It opened $2.75 lower and finished down $3.62. That's about a 25% loss in one day and 40% off the highs. Where were the experts who should have been getting you out when it was trading at 17, 18, and 19 dollars a share? That "Outperform" must mean "get-me-the-hell-out" considering it closed at $12.

I am not picking on these specific brokerage houses. They are ALL equally bad. Their recommendations and research are garbage. Don't read it and don't listen to anything they tell you. They don't know! They prove that with their recommendations.

It makes me very angry when I see how badly you are treated. I watch the talking heads on CNBC-TV; sometimes I even listen. That's when I get livid. I shouldn't listen. One big brokerage house after another has watched some stock fall 50% and now they are changing their recommendation from "Buy" to "Hold". What is the matter with their so called "experts" who let you lose 50% of your investment in stock after stock before they tell you not to buy any more of these losers? And when it finally bottoms out another 30% or 40% lower, they say it is time to switch to a better issue. They never tell you to sell except when it goes to loss. They NEVER tell you to put in a stop. *These are the analysts who are literally paid millions to help you go broke.* Please! I am gagging. That is why I tell you never to listen to any broker. I guarantee he will not tell you what I have because he will put himself out of business. Besides, he doesn't even know he doesn't know. He thinks he is an expert. YUK! Let me get off this soapbox.

Remember the basic premise, "If it doesn't go up, don't buy it".

GOVERNMENT STATISTICS

Here is some research you can do every day — if you want to waste your time. There are daily releases of government statistics and reports that make the market move — sometimes quite violently. Please, please don't pay any attention to them. For each statistic released this month there is a revision about 30 days later. Many times the revision is from 50% to 500% different from the original number, yet when that number came out, the market reacted like a scorched dog. I have seen auto sales go from an original 1% increase "estimate" to a revised actual number the next month being 1.8% increase. How can you be off 80%? Second quarter GDP for 1997 was estimated to be 2.2%; later it was revised to 3.6%. Off by 50%! 50%? How about this one: June 1997 drug store sales were estimated to increase 0.3% but the actual figure was later "revised" to up 1.2% — only 400% off! What are *you* going to do with all this wonderful "research"? What are they doing in Washington? Sticking their finger out the window! You know the old formula — GI=GO — garbage in equals garbage out. You are getting garbage so just ignore it. Unfortunately, these are your tax dollars turning into garbage.

We are all told that Federal Reserve Chairman Alan Greenspan knows all about everything financial. In 1996 he predicted the GDP growth would be between 2.0% and 2.5% in 1997 and added that consumer prices would rise between 2.75% to 3.5%. GDP was 3.9% and consumer prices were up only 1.7%. Both off more than 40%. Greenspan and all his money puppets *could not even come close*. These are the geniuses who are trying to micromanage our economy.

I doubt if any big-shot research analysts will ever read this book, but I'll take a shot anyway. I recommend that researchers find the best performing industry first and then find the best companies within that group. Buy one or maybe two or three of those issues. I don't care how good a company's stock is it will not go up to any great extent unless the whole group moves.

Researchers should spend more time trying to predict overall industry trends and their synergistic effect on each other and the general economy rather than analyzing individual stocks.

ECONOMISTS

The last guy you ever want to listen to is an economist. They have a head full of theory and most of them have never had a real job where making money was the yardstick of success. They will quote you formulas and econometrics (that's just more formidable formulas which predict what will happen to the economy and which only other economists seem to *think* they understand) and all that other useless stuff. None of it will show up in your checkbook. Economists argue with each other over their various theories and seem to forget that they are *theories* and not practical applications. Keynesian economic theory has been taught in college for 50 years and now it is out the window, but many economists still think it is true. Don't ask an economist what the price is for a loaf of bread and quart of milk because they don't know. Being an economist is the only job I know of where you can be wrong all of the time and not get fired.

SYSTEMS, SEMINARS & SOFTWARE

I used to have a commodity broker when I owned my brokerage company who made up great sounding systems and sold them for $3,000 each. Bank checks only, thank you. Of course, they were sold with a 100% money back guarantee, but that doesn't cover your losses. One time he was using one of his systems and made $150,000 in one month. I called him and said, "Mike, you have made a big profit. It's time to take a vacation. Get your head straight." "Don't worry, Al, I know what I'm doing." Not a chance. The very next month he was using the same system and lost $155,000. He is still selling this method and only shows you the month he made the $150,000.

Don't be a seminar junkie or a systems nerd. So often I have seen customers who have paid big money for this nonsense, bring it home and think they can "tweak" the system to make it work even better. Please! If it was any good the seller wouldn't need your money.

Maybe you own or are considering buying some of that sophisticated software into which you can put 10, 20 or 30 parameters and have it pick out just exactly the stock or commodity that will make you a fortune. Mañana. Maybe. Here is a basic rule — the more complicated the system, and the more parameters you have, the *less* likely it will work.

One more point about systems. They love to talk about optimization. All this means is you must change the 'system' to conform to current conditions. The problem is you won't recognize what 'current' conditions are until they are over with and gone bye- bye. Any good method of trading will work at all times and fit any market without 'optimization'. This is another big word to confuse you and separate you from your money. Basic technical analysis in its simplest form works best. What I have shown you in this book will work *all* the time, no tweaking necessary.

Follow the KISS formula — you know, "**K**eep **I**t **S**imple **S**tupid". There are some very simple methods of trading. What I call 'best' means very simple — few computations and easy to follow without a lot of your time. Simple. Simple! Simple!!

Another cutie to run price up is the dog and pony show called 'in-depth research analysis' by some big name promoter who advertises in a national paper about a free meeting. At the free meeting their research analysts will tell you about how to pick a good stock and do research analysis so you can get rich. He says he is showing you how their system works and they want you to subscribe to their newsletter or something like that. Hidden in all this falderall he keeps mentioning Therapeutic Biofonics (I made that up in case there really is a company by that name). They show you why this company is undervalued and why this $1.20 stock is really worth $26. In a matter of weeks, a really good manipulator can run up a stock 200% to 5,000% until he runs out of "greater fools". Also these promoters will have private and public meetings for stockbrokers, investment bankers, mutual fund managers, pension fund managers, etc. — the money people. They will put out a slick color research brochure on the company that they wrote and have the president or CEO speak and answer questions. The next day these dupes will start telling their clients about the wonderful investment meeting and what they learned. These con men own thousands of shares of this stock at a fraction of the price it is offered and will be selling to you at the highest price possible. There are millions of dollars here, but not for you.

If you want to play the game (and I don't recommend it unless you are a professional) you need to know if this is their first or second meeting and how many meetings they plan. These promotions are usually over in 60 days. You will need to follow the price and volume action every day. Ride it up and be ready to get out. It is called 'pump and dump' and is also done by the day traders on the Internet. Once the touts abandon it it will fall to its true level. I saw one stock go from 50 cents to $6.00 and back down again to 50 cents. I won't do it. You must be an "insider". Yes, I know it is illegal, but they do it so cleverly in the name of "research" that they stay within the limits of the law. More proof that research is BS.

The great gurus of Wall Street are constantly referring to "valuation". Some stock is selling for a certain price and it is "undervalued" and therefore must go up. Why? Who decides what "valuation" means? It is like having two or more people tell me which perfume smells best. Each one of these gurus has his own definition of "valuation". You may not know what the real value of a stock is today, but do you want to buy it to find out? Don't listen to the hype about any stock being "undervalued". That could be a costly exercise. If it was at $45 and today it is $20 does that mean it was "overvalued" at $45 and today it is "undervalued"? Maybe it will drop to $10. This is the nonsensical logic that market experts use to unload these poor issues on you, the general public.

Let's not make it complicated. What a stock is selling for today is what its value is today. There is no such thing as *true* "valuation" because *all* valuation is in the mind of the beholder. You know, beauty is in the eye of the beholder.

Please don't try to emulate some big name like Warren Buffett. You can't. You are not in his league. Neither am I! If you don't have several million bucks you can't trade the way he does and if you are reading this book I know you can't do what he does. The latest was his huge purchase of silver in 1998. It was announced and the silver market took off for the moon. Now it is heading back to new low prices.

My personal bet (and I can't prove it) is that Mr. Buffett sold enough of his original silver portfolio near those artificial highs caused by the emotional

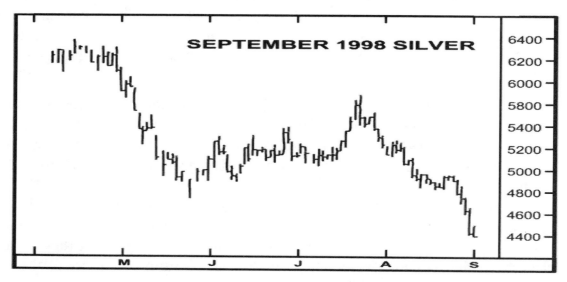

furor of his announced buying and he now has all his money back from the low price purchase and still has a few tons of "free" silver. Don't coattail someone who is not in your class. Do your own thing.

Those "hypothetical" projections of big profits you see all the time in advertising — don't believe a word. Only believe real time actual copies of statements from brokerage houses and then be sure to call them to confirm they have not been 'doctored'. The hypothetical figures do not take into account things like slippage and commission. For example, your stop on September gold is 298 and the market opens at 296 and you are filled at 294 because of the wide opening range. This is common. That extra $400/contract loss never shows up in the hypothetical computations.

TRADING

One of the key trading rules: you must *have the discipline to stay with your method*. If it is something new, you should then paper trade it for at least 3 to 6 months before you put your real hard-earned bucks on it. Don't be concerned about having losses. Most of the good traders I know only win about 40% of the time, but their losses are always small. They maintain a 3 to 1 profit to loss ratio. That means for every $1 they lose they win $3. Even with a 40% win ration you can see this will make a ton of money.

Stay with your system. Especially when you get one of those brilliant flashes which violates your method but where you know you are absolutely, positively sure this is the greatest winner of all times. What you can be sure of is that this is going to turn into your worst nightmare. You will become emotionally attached to it and won't get out as you know you should. Hindsight is always 20/20.

Speaking of emotions, there is a tremendous difference in "paper" trading and real trading, with *your* money at risk. Things will look different to you then. You will either act too quickly or not quickly enough. You'll see.

You will have to learn patience. When you see something really good you don't have to jump on it immediately. Acting too soon is a costly bad habit. If it is good today it will be good tomorrow and you might want to sleep on it. Sometimes I will see a situation developing and I know it isn't quite ready. I just watch it and when it breaks out I go with it even if I have to pay a little more. Get positive confirmation that you are right. Let the market tell you; don't you tell the market. The market is never wrong, but you are.

You might also want to sneak into a position slowly. Maybe you want to buy 500 shares of a certain stock. Buy 100 to start and add to it as your analysis is confirmed. Average up! Don't go for broke with all your money on one horse in one race. If there are eight races, plan to spread your money around with that same amount bet on each race.

Whatever amount you start with in your portfolio, consider what your goal is for the year, not for each trade. If you want to make 100% on your money (which I consider very reasonable for a commodity or stock option player) don't worry if you have some losses. You will. Look at the long run and you will see your cash increasing over several months. In January my trading account dropped 15%, but I didn't panic. I eliminated the losing positions and bought others and by the end of February the account had increased 33%.

When I came back to trading after several years off it took me a while to get back into the long-term discipline.

Discipline, Patience and Stops are your three best friends.

Money. It really gets your head turned around. Making a lot of money is just as upsetting to you as losing a lot of money. When I was a floor trader and made a good hit I would take a vacation. I usually took about six or eight short vacations per year and always took the month of December off. That's how I met my wife — while I was on one of my vacations. That was a winning trade!

Another thing, when you make a good profit reward yourself — buy yourself a gift like a nice piece of jewelry or a new car. This is important psychologically as it bolsters you mentally, building your self-confidence.

You have heard the "market climbs a wall of worry". As long as there are a lot of bears around the market will continue to go up. There are many really good technical indicators, but none of them will give the exact top (or bottom) day of the turn in the market. The great soothsayers of markets are more wrong than right. Don't worry about either the top or bottom day. The safest part of the market is that 60% to 80% in the middle.

Fundamentals are important. They tell you all about how the company is doing financially as you read the annual report for the company, but this document is about a year old when you get it. As far as I'm concerned, it is ancient history, prehistoric.

Commodity fundamentals such as the number of cattle or hogs on feed or the weather for the South American soybean crop are somewhat more timely, but they don't give you the right time or place to put on your position. I have personally not known a pure fundamentalist who has made money, but I'm sure there are some.

Combining *both* fundamentals and technical indicators can be very positive. The problem with fundamentals is the market does not make a nice even stairstep up (or down) to your projected price. The zigs and the zags can make you a nervous wreck; you will probably get so emotional you will be selling the lows and buying the highs. To be a successful trader (and I don't want you to be a trader), you must learn everything you can about technical analysis. In my opinion everything known about a stock or commodity is reflected in the last tick. Learn to understand these price changes by reading the chart and you won't have to know anything about the fundamentals.

Many times I will buy a stock or stock option and have absolutely no idea what they do, where they are located, the size of the company or anything. My stockbroker laughs at me, but he never fades me. A few days later I might look them up. Recently I bought one with a name that sounded like a bank and found out the following week it was a large funeral home chain. Who cares? I made money in it.

LIMITED PARTNERSHIPS

I want to mention Limited Partnerships, telecommunications, oil deals and other "inside deals". Don't. Just don't! Ninety-five percent or more go broke. Just because it has some big names in it doesn't mean it is going to make money. The big names were conned or given some kind of inside deal just to use their name. The General Partner has 100% control of *your* money. If you decide to sell, who is going to buy your share? Don't look at me; I know better.

Some highbinder is going to come to you with a great story and tell you all about the "smart money people" who are buying into this deal. You know, movie stars, sports figures, radio talk show hosts, etc. "It won't last long; you have to act now or there won't be any of this left." I guarantee it is a loser. Little guys never get a smell of the "smart money deals". If they want your little cash it can't be any good. Maybe even a friend will say he is getting into this and will want to do you a favor and let you in too. With friends like that you don't need enemies.

When I was a broker, I would get calls out of the blue from someone I never heard of who had a boatload of oil or sugar or something and he had to get it sold because it was on the high seas and would be in port in two weeks. He wants me to sell it for him for a piece of the action, but he needs a letter of credit from my bank to consummate the sale.

Think about this. I'm a nobody-broker working at a no-name clearinghouse and he is going to let me in on this great deal. Please, I wasn't born in a barn. And there are still dummies falling for this today. Now a great number of them are coming out of Nigeria. These people have made scam a science.

Later on I became a promoter and started putting deals together, forming corporations, writing prospectuses and Limited Partnerships, etc. The use of the word promoters is not politically correct any more. Now they call themselves venture capitalists. Same thing.

Don't put your money in any small venture capital pool and you can't get into the big ones unless you have big money. There are exceptions to this rule; however, if you want to violate it, you will be the one to take the consequences. This is part of that hard-learned rule to *keep control of your money.*

One of my best commodity customers was a very rich cattleman and I grew to know him well. He told me about an oil deal he was going into and as a favor to me he said I could get in for $5,000 per share. He was an honest man so I sent the oil promoters $10,000. That was the last I saw of my $10 'Gs' and I didn't even get kissed. He was a limited partner the same as I and he lost a lot more than I did, but it is still gone. I did not blame him. I blame me. Live and learn. Keep control.

INITIAL PUBLIC OFFERINGS

A word about IPO's — Initial Public Offerings. Same thing. Don't! Your broker calls you. He has been given "a limited number of shares of this hot new issue that is coming out next Thursday and his boss has allowed him to allocate 500 shares to you. Don't miss out on this, Mr. Mushroom, as it is going to double in the next year and might become the next Intel and you wouldn't want to miss that. This is so good I am buying it for my own account". Yeah! Remember those pigs — the ones that fly.

If you are a small trader (have less than one million dollars in your account, yeah, that's what small means), you are not even going to get a sniff of any really good IPO. Some representative from the new issue company may get on a conference call with all the brokers and give them the hype about "all the great potential this company has because they have a new method of extracting gold from sea water (some con man actually tried to sell me that one). You guys can really do your customers a favor by getting them a few shares at this once-in-a-lifetime offering". Please, I can't stand it. Those good ones are for the million dollar accounts. The only one you will ever get a shot at is some unknown dog that will probably be selling for one half its original offering price next year — the ones the big boys don't want. The percentage of IPO's that make money is very small. You may miss the very occasional good one, but that is no loss. Remember my word for IPO's is 'don't'.

There are literally thousands of books about the stock and commodity markets in general and thousands more about how some guy got rich who is going to tell you his system. He probably did do it and he knows how to keep on doing it, but he also has probably devoted his life to this. You must do the same if you want to make money the way he did.

I not only am showing you how to do it, but can prove everything I say. See the certified statement in the back of the book from my CPA who has verified every trade I made during 1998.

Remember the story about the lady who came up to the great pianist Chopin after a concert and said to him, "I'd give half my life to be able to play the way you do". And he replied, "Madam, I have given my *whole* life". Don't go wasting your money buying these books; you can get most of them at the library for free. Better yet, check out a western or detective story.

I love those movies about Wall Street where you see the inner machinations of the big corporate empires with all the in-fighting for money and power. Great fun. More truth than fiction, but you aren't there and probably never will be. Learn some basics and be happy making 30% to 50% per year on your money while protecting your capital during bad times. It's not that hard and it is a lot easier on your nerves.

You will have a very substantial income by following the recommendations outlined here and you will have many "taxable events". That means you owe the IRS, as they are your partner in all the profitable trades. You get to keep the losses. Many financial planners and brokers will tell you that you need to be in "tax sheltered situations". Usually some special deal he is selling. I have rarely seen one that ever paid more than if you had been in a non-tax-sheltered investment which netted you a lot more than if you had just paid the taxes. Do the numbers yourself or have your accountant help you. Personally I'll take the gross profits and pay the IRS. You can't hide from them because every transaction is recorded at the brokerage house. *Don't try.* Just pay them and sleep at night, but pay only what is legally required.

There is one legal way to get around paying taxes on money made with this program. Open a tax-deferred account like an IRA or trade in your current tax-deferred 401K account if you have one. This is not my field of expertise so I can only refer you to any experienced CPA who has done this many times. Whatever he charges you will be more than made up in the taxes you will save. Any discount brokerage house will open an IRA at no cost.

I've been a trader for more than 35 years (starting with stocks, then commodity futures, now stock options and mutual funds). I bought a seat on the Chicago Open Board of Trade in 1964 so I could act as a floor trader to trade my personal account. In 1984 I founded and built one of the largest introducing commodity brokerage companies, with 35 branch offices, called *The World Trading Group*. All that has brought me to this conclusion (which applies even more to the stock market industry where they like to appear to be respectable): *No one gives a hoot about the little investor* except the regulators who just are doing a job. They don't understand the business of making money. *That is what this book is all about — helping you, the little guy, make your money grow, safely.*

I haven't stressed safety at all because it is such an integrated and integral part of this method. When I talk about safety, I mean the way to protect your capital from a big loss for any reason. I believe the mutual fund trading method outlined here is the safest way to invest your money at any time, no matter what the market conditions happen to be. You now know how to recognize a bull market and in which mutual funds to be invested. You now know how to recognize a bear market and to be in cash (or short) to protect yourself from losing what you made in the last bull market. You control your money at all times. That's safety.

There are a few, very few, good market letters out there. Most are too sophisticated and too complicated for the person with less than $250,000. I have read many of them over the years and, again, I don't think they know what they don't know. I love the ones with the money back guarantee. That doesn't apply to the money you lost on their recommendations or the money you could have made following the simple principles laid down here.

I do subscribe to one market letter just to get a world's eye view of what is going on, but I rarely pick the same stocks or mutual funds that he does. Bert Dohmen's *Wellington Financial Letter* is extremely good. Send for a sample copy. Bert uses common sense. I've known him for 25 years and respect his opinions.

I use first names of people I have known over the years to keep from being sued. Many of them would not like my telling how they made their money. Many other wonderful people are also referred to on a first name basis only since I haven't asked permission for their names to be included in this book.

Personally, I don't think you should be trading individual issues unless you can make at least 100% annually on your money. In commodities you should make 200%. When I did trade commodities, I always made at least 400% and more with my personal account, but I don't trade commodities any more as I don't want to put in the time. Stocks and stock options can make you a lot of money. Trading is *very* time consuming and requires a great deal of effort and experience along with total concentration.

Mutual funds are best for the little guy provided you do as I suggest in the mutual fund chapter of this book. It is brutally easy, takes very little time and you can sleep nights because you don't have to worry about which way the market is going. You will always be on the right side of it.

I want to discourage you from trying to pick stocks by the usual method of "research" because there is a way you can build and keep a successful portfolio of winners all the time *when you are in a bull market*, but it will require some (not a lot) of work on your part. Yes, I can criticize people who can't; however, that criticism is hollow if I can't give you something better and here it is.

First, I must assume you have some money, maybe $15,000 or more. It is possible to do it with a lot less. Buy an issue of *Investor's Business Daily* and look in the section called *Investor's Business Daily Industry Prices* (they are actually ratings of a whole group of similar companies) usually found near the back of Section One on the page with all the Market Index charts. Here you find a list of 197 industry groups ranked by performance for the last 3 months, one week ago and today. That is the one you want, not the ranking of 6 months. The amount of money you have will determine how many groups you wish to use for your stock selection. Let's assume you have enough money to be able to buy 100 shares of 5 different stocks at an average price of $30 per share. Yes, you can buy less than 100 shares which is called an odd lot; however, commissions are higher and they compute to a higher percentage. Sometimes you may have to give up a 1/16 or 1/8 of a point extra.

Pick out the top five industry groups; each day they might be slightly different, but you are concerned with this day. These are the groups with the upward momentum. What you are doing here is following a basic law of physics: *a body in motion tends to remain in motion in the direction in which it is*

Investor's Business Daily Industry Prices

197 Industry Groups are ranked 1 through 197 on price performance of all stocks in the industry in the latest 6 months (1 = best performance). Top ten industries in performance yesterday are boldface. Worst 10 are underlined.

Rank This Wk	Rank Last Fri.	3 Mo. Ago	Industry Name	No. of Stocks In Grp	% Chg. Since Jan.1	Daily % Chg.
1	1	13	Computer-Local Networks	54	+51.0	+0.7
2	2	5	Elec-Laser Sys/Component	32	103.6	+0.2
3	3	12	Elec-Semiconductor Mfg	89	+62.8	+1.0
4	4	10	Telecommunications-Equip	159	+48.2	+0.6
5	5	11	Retail-Consumer Elect	14	+86.0	+0.9
6	6	80	Oil & Gas-Drilling	18	+59.2	+0.7
7	7	25	Elec-Misc Components	51	+42.2	+0.5
8	8	60	Oil&Gas-Cdn Exp&Prod	94	+39.5	+0.5
9	9	15	Telecommunctns-Cellulr	36	+51.5	+0.5
10	10	121	Oil&Gas-U S Explo&Prod	110	+34.4	+1.6
11	11	28	Computer-Peripheral Eq	71	+20.3	-0.6
12	12	101	Energy-Other	22	+33.6	+0.5
13	13	9	Computer Softwre-Desktop	37	+39.4	+1.3
14	14	67	Computer-Memory Devices	42	+20.1	+0.4
15	15	31	Medical-Generic Drugs	16	+11.8	+0.4
16	16	83	Oil&Gas-Field Services	38	+23.0	+0.7
17	17	108	Oil&Gas-Machinery/Equip	19	+43.8	+1.2
18	**18**	**33**	**Medical-Biomed/Genetics**	**172**	**+28.7**	**+2.7**
19	19	8	Media-Cable Tv	19	+57.9	0.0
20	20	22	Elec Products-Misc	65	+26.2	+1.0
21	21	111	Mining-Gems	19	+34.8	0.0
22	22	7	Telecommunications-Svcs	110	+39.6	-0.6
23	23	82	Household-Audio/Video	12	+17.4	+0.4
24	24	27	Leisure-Gaming	65	+23.7	+0.4
25	25	20	Media-Radio/Tv	38	+25.6	+0.6
26	26	29	Bldg Prod-Wood	12	+21.5	-1.3
27	27	76	Elec-Measrng Instruments	36	+26.9	+0.7
28	28	51	Computer Softwr-Enterpse	195	+0.7	+1.0
29	**29**	**90**	**Consumer Products-Misc**	**39**	**+3.2**	**+1.8**
30	30	3	Internet-Software	39	+54.2	-0.7
31	31	46	Chemicals-Plastics	27	+22.2	+0.3
32	32	125	Oil&Gas-U S Integrated	11	+17.8	+0.8
33	**33**	**87**	**Oil&Gas-Intl Specialty**	**3**	**+22.5**	**+2.3**
34	34	19	Shoes & Rel Apparel	27	+41.3	-3.3
35	35	16	Retail/Wholesale-Jewelry	19	+30.7	-0.4
36	36	34	Paper & Paper Products	33	+8.0	-0.1
37	37	68	Oil&Gas-Cdn Integrated	7	+32.0	+1.0
38	38	94	Electrical-Equipment	22	+20.4	-0.9
39	39	55	Machinery-Const/Mining	10	+26.2	+0.1
40	40	52	Elec-Scientific Instrumn	31	+21.9	+0.7
41	41	88	Metal Proc & Fabrication	50	+9.0	+0.8
42	42	6	Finance-Investment Bkrs	39	+36.2	-1.6
43	43	64	Medical-Products	131	+10.6	+1.1
44	44	195	Elec-Parts Distributors	16	-1.6	-0.6
45	45	144	Retail-Discount&Variety	12	+11.5	+1.2
46	46	37	Computer Softw-Educ/Entr	18	+7.1	+0.7
47	47	44	Household-Appliances	11	+19.4	-0.4
48	48	61	Retail-Home Furnishings	19	+7.5	-0.3
49	49	24	Finance-Consumr/Comml	40	+24.3	-1.0
50	**50**	**50**	**Elec-Semiconductor Equip**	**60**	**+37.1**	**+2.7**
51	51	98	Metal Ores-Non Ferrous	8	+27.8	-0.6
52	52	97	Pollution Control-Svcs	68	+0.7	-0.1
53	53	65	Oil&Gas-Intl Integrated	6	+13.9	+1.1
54	54	43	Leisure-Hotels & Motels	34	+10.7	-0.3
55	55	103	Medical-Instruments	91	+1.8	+0.2
56	56	109	Comml Svcs-Security/Sfty	60	-5.4	+0.9
57	57	39	Comml Services-Misc	150	+11.2	+1.0
58	58	79	Pollution Control-Equip	32	+17.8	+1.0
59	59	194	Comml Serv-Business Svcs	28	-12.5	+1.1
60	60	17	Computer Software-Fin	30	+8.2	-0.3
61	61	115	Electrical-Control Instr	17	+16.3	+0.3
62	62	171	Electrical-Connectors	11	+12.3	+0.7
63	63	173	Utility-Gas Distribution	47	+5.0	+0.4
64	64	78	Machinery-Farm	11	+28.4	-0.3
65	65	63	Auto Mfrs-Foreign	8	+29.7	+0.7
66	66	69	Leisure-Movies & Related	42	+3.6	+0.1
67	67	49	Computer-Manufacturers	20	+40.9	-0.5
68	68	100	Auto/Truck-Original Eqp	38	+12.3	-0.4
69	69	38	Trucks & Parts-Hvy Duty	13	+30.5	-0.8
70	70	71	Chemicals-Basic	12	+22.0	+0.8
71	71	48	Steel-Producers	19	+11.8	+1.2
72	72	56	Finance-Publ Inv Fd-Frn	151	+11.6	+0.3
73	73	161	Leisure-Photo Equip/Rel	10	+14.0	-0.5
74	74	128	Computer-Integrated Syst	46	+0.3	+0.8
75	75	86	Transportation-Truck	43	+6.0	+0.5
76	76	84	Bldg-Constr Prods/Misc	45	+11.0	-0.3
77	77	163	Transportation-Equip Mfg	16	+11.0	+0.3
78	78	42	Utility-Telephone	17	+17.5	-0.4
79	79	168	Retail-Super/Mini Mkts	34	-2.0	-0.1
80	80	70	Bldg-Paint & Allied Prds	12	+7.0	+0.3
81	81	36	Leisure-Services	43	+14.7	+0.3
82	82	57	Retail-Restaurants	109	+7.7	+0.1
83	83	127	Household-Housewares	12	+18.0	+0.8
84	84	59	Metal Ores-Misc	12	+2.0	-0.2
85	85	123	Oil&Gas-Prod/Pipeline	23	+14.4	+0.3
86	86	131	Aerospace/Defense	10	+14.8	-0.1
87	87	54	Transportation-Svcs	12	+23.3	0.0
88	88	146	Bldg-A/C & Heating Prds	16	+7.3	+0.2
89	89	107	Computer Software-Med	19	+7.9	+0.6
90	90	102	Medical/Dental/Serv	61	-10.9	-0.3
91	91	118	Chemicals-Specialty	64	+3.6	+0.6
92	92	135	Bldg-Heavy Const	18	+6.4	+0.7
93	93	124	Hsehold/Office Furniture	26	+5.6	+0.7
94	94	18	Retail-Apparel/Shoe	59	+16.5	+0.8
95	95	104	Comml Svcs-Printing	21	-9.5	-0.5
96	96	81	Aerospace/Defense Eqp	49	+3.3	+0.1
97	97	160	Utility-Water Supply	16	+6.2	+0.8
98	**98**	**4**	**Internet-Ntwk Sec/Sltns**	**33**	**+85.8**	**+1.7**
99	99	21	Financial Services-Misc	34	+19.3	-1.2
100	100	175	Transportation-Ship	7	-6.6	+0.1
101	101	113	Containers	29	+2.3	+0.4
102	102	106	Comml-Leasing Cos	37	-0.3	-0.5
103	103	155	Agricultural Operations	31	+4.3	+0.1
104	104	182	Banks-West/Southwest	102	+0.1	0.0
105	105	47	Leisure-Products	53	+0.1	+0.4
106	106	95	Diversified Operations	57	+1.8	-0.4
107	107	105	Elec-Military Systems	31	+9.3	+0.7
108	108	99	Insurance-Brokers	9	+17.3	+0.3
109	109	66	Retail/Whlsle-Cmptr/Cell	36	-5.1	-1.6
110	110	45	Comml Svcs-Advertising	24	-6.9	0.0
111	111	58	Retail-Misc/Diversified	87	-12.3	-0.7
112	112	73	Office-Equip & Automatn	11	-2.2	+0.1
113	113	174	Banks-Midwest	103	+0.0	+0.2
114	114	126	Transportation-Rail	13	+8.5	-0.2
115	115	72	Machinery-Gen Industrial	51	+7.5	0.0
116	116	185	Steel-Specialty Alloys	13	-2.6	-0.8
117	117	130	Media-Newspapers	18	+4.8	-0.2
118	118	77	Computer-Services	100	-4.9	-0.1
119	119	147	Office Supplies Mfg	22	+1.2	+0.4
120	120	151	Oil&Gas-Refining/Mktg	33	+2.4	-0.5
121	121	179	Medical-Outpnt/Hm Care	33	-22.4	-0.4
122	122	152	Medical-Hlth Maint Org	22	-0.6	+0.1
123	123	157	Insurance-Life	38	-3.2	-0.5
124	124	35	Banks-Money Center	4	+16.8	-2.8
125	125	132	Food-Dairy Products	11	-8.1	-0.3
126	126	129	Medical/Dental-Supplies	42	-6.5	+0.3
127	127	74	Metal Ores-Gold/Silver	19	-4.0	-1.6
128	128	138	Retail/Whlsle-Bldg Prods	21	+0.1	-0.3
129	129	136	Finance-Investment Mgmt	36	-5.9	-1.8
130	130	177	Oil & Gas-U S Royalty Tr	17	+10.3	+0.5
131	131	134	Real Estate Development	20	+9.4	+0.1
132	132	149	Finance-Savings & Loan	269	+0.3	+0.2
133	133	110	Retail-Department Stores	16	+3.1	-1.7
134	134	145	Medical-Ethical Drugs	83	-15.5	+0.9
135	135	166	Bldg-Mobile/Mfg & Rv	29	-9.3	-1.5
136	136	62	Textile-Apparel Mfg	58	-8.7	+0.7
137	**137**	**193**	**Computer-Optical Recogn**	**16**	**+2.7**	**+1.8**
138	138	176	Finance-Mortgage Reit	40	-2.6	-0.4
139	139	40	Banks-Foreign	47	-2.1	+0.4
140	140	85	Transportation-Airline	25	+4.9	-0.2
141	141	23	Retail-Mail Order&Direct	33	-10.5	-0.4
142	142	114	Finance-Mrtg&Rel Svc	38	-3.9	-0.9
143	143	117	Fin-Pub Trd Inv Fd-Eqt	58	+4.5	-0.3
144	144	172	Beverages-Soft Drinks	12	-7.0	-0.4
145	145	41	Leisure-Toys/Games/Hobby	24	+13.1	-0.7
146	146	170	Utility-Electric Power	88	-6.4	-0.5
147	147	183	Comml Serv-Staffing	46	-15.2	+0.8
148	148	1	Internet-E..commerce	59	+27.0	-1.3
149	149	164	Insurance-Prop/Cas/Titl	116	-7.4	+0.1
150	150	92	Banks-Super Regional	25	-3.2	-1.8
151	151	143	Food-Meat Products	14	-24.2	-2.5
152	152	154	Metal Prod-Fasteners	7	+0.6	-0.4
153	153	26	Insurance-Acc & Health	10	-3.7	+0.6
154	154	133	Real Estate Operations	40	+4.9	0.0
155	155	189	Food-Misc Preparation	55	-8.8	-0.2
156	156	14	Media-Periodicals	13	+12.9	+0.2
157	157	116	Cosmetics/Personal Care	63	-9.1	-0.4
158	158	139	Banks-Northeast	172	-1.7	+0.3
159	159	91	Bldg-Hand Tools	9	+0.0	-0.9
160	160	93	Metal Prod-Distributor	7	-1.6	+1.4
161	161	148	Beverages-Alcoholic	23	-5.7	+0.7
162	162	140	Retail/Whlse Office Supl	10	-8.4	+0.5
163	163	2	Internet-Isp/Content	78	+78.1	-0.8
164	164	165	Finance-Equity Reit	176	-1.9	+0.8
165	165	32	Retail-Major Disc Chains	7	+10.1	-1.6
166	166	186	Retail/Wholesale-Food	19	-6.8	+0.5
167	167	75	Computer-Graphics	19	+0.8	-0.6
168	168	178	Auto/Truck-Replace Prts	22	-6.1	+0.4
169	169	142	Bldg-Resident/Commrcl	34	-9.5	-0.1
170	170	191	Food-Flour & Grain	7	-12.2	-0.9
171	171	30	Transport-Air Freight	13	+3.0	+0.2
172	172	122	Medical-Drug/Diversified	5	-1.7	-1.7
173	**173**	**119**	**Medical-Whsle Drg/Sund**	**19**	**-17.4**	**+2.2**
174	174	162	Machine-Tools & Rel Prod	23	-6.7	+0.4
175	175	120	Bldg-Cement/Concrt/Ag	15	+1.8	-0.3
176	176	150	Machinery-Mtl Hdlg/Autmn	18	-9.1	+0.4
177	177	159	Banks-Southeast	139	-6.1	-0.2
178	178	112	Insurance-Diversified	4	+10.0	-1.3
179	179	89	Media-Books	17	-6.1	-0.6
180	180	187	Tobacco	10	-21.0	+0.4
181	181	137	Soap & Clng Preparatns	9	+3.7	+1.5
182	182	141	Auto/Truck-Tires & Misc	7	-2.3	+0.4
183	183	169	Textile-Mill/Hsehold	29	-18.1	-0.9
184	184	158	Food-Confectionery	8	-5.1	-0.4
185	185	190	Food-Canned	9	-9.4	0.0
186	186	53	Computer Softwr-Security	12	-12.8	+0.5
187	**187**	**188**	**Bldg-Maintenance & Svc**	**14**	**-11.7**	**+1.9**
188	188	167	Chemicals-Fertilizers	7	-3.4	+0.7
189	189	180	Fin-Pub Trd Inv Fd-Bond	338	-5.7	0.0
190	190	196	Retail-Drug Stores	8	-21.1	-1.6
191	**191**	**153**	**Comml Svcs-Linen Supply**	**5**	**-8.4**	**+1.6**
192	192	156	Retail/Whlsle-Auto Parts	17	-9.1	-0.8
193	**193**	**184**	**Medical-Hospitals**	**13**	**-33.8**	**+1.6**
194	194	192	Funeral Svcs & Rel	6	-29.7	+0.9
195	195	181	Comml Svcs-Schools	26	-21.8	0.0
196	196	96	Auto Mfrs-Domestic	3	-14.7	-6.1
197	197	197	Medical-Nursing Homes	24	-46.9	+0.2
0	0	0	S & P Industrial Index		+9.2	-0.7
0	0	0	S & P 500 Index		+8.1	-0.9

moving. For example, they might be *Computer Software-Internet, Retail-Apparel/Shoe, Finance- Investment Management, Retail-Consumer Electric and Media-Cable TV*. (See the above exhibit.) This is the easy part. Now you have to do some work.

Every stock falls into some category. From each category you want to select one stock from that group. Under the *Transportation-Truck* category you will usually find more than 15 or 20 stocks. These can be found occasionally listed under *Industry Group* Focus (See the above exhibit.) in *Investor's*

Industry Group Focus: Computer Software — Enterprise
Stocks shown by total of their EPS and RS ranks; o or a after symbol means OTC or Amex.

Rank	Stock	Trade Symbol	EPS Rtg	REL STR	Acc Dis	Recnt Price	% off High Price	PE Ratio	5yr PE Hi - lo		Shrs Outstd (mill)	Avg. DlyVol (100s)	Last Qtr. EPS	Last Qtr. Sales	Annual Net % Margin	Annual ROE	Year % Debt	Beta
1	Siebel Systems Inc	SEBL o	99	95	B	59.31	12	76	113	27	91.1	14382	+100	+ 83	18.7	22.3	0	+1.69
2	Veritas Software Corp	VRTS o	99	93	B	55.25	13	91	104	15	165.6	21451	+ 43	+138	28.4	39.3	0	+2.22
3	Clarify Inc	CLFY o	98	94	C	32.06	46	65	234	15	22.8	5373	+180	+ 75	8.9	11.4	0	+3.48
4	Electronics For Imaging	EFII o	96	95	B	53.13	12	38	50	10	53.8	8312	+223	+ 41	15.7	12.5	1	+1.96
5	Legato Systems Inc	LGTO o	99	91	A	71.56	14	78	122	17	40.6	8793	+222	+ 65	29.0	20.4	0	+1.18
6	Project Software & Dev	PSDI o	94	95	A	42.75	14	24	59	8	10.0	1336	+ 19	+ 17	12.1	19.7	0	+2.93
7	Oracle Corp	ORCL o	97	91	B	38.13	7	43	52	18	1439.5	....	+ 33	+ 22	15.0	35.9	10	+1.56
8	Adobe Systems Inc	ADBE o	93	95	B	85.38	9	35	42	14	61.0	9935	+ 63	+ 8	18.7	20.5	0	+1.37
9	Citrix Systems Inc	CTXS o	99	83	B	50.88	22	51	196	10	87.3	14396	+164	+ 68	38.4	26.3	0	+1.38
10	Remedy Corp	RMDY o	96	84	C	21.06	62	27	125	11	29.0	4329	+ 31	+ 45	18.8	13.6	0	+1.71
11	National Instrument Corp	NATI o	92	88	A	44.38	8	36	39	16	33.1	1056	+ 22	+ 18	20.4	20.7	2	+1.43
12	Unigraphics Solutions	UGS	85	95	A	25.50	2	31	31	9	36.3	260	+ 19	+ 22	1.9	33.8	62	+2.58
13	Micromuse Inc	MUSE o	82	94	C	46.50	23	116	488	52	15.9	1812	+999	+103	− 2.4	− 2.0	1	+4.02
14	Synopsys Inc	SNPS o	94	81	A	59.19	6	25	210	13	70.9	7671	+ 35	+ 15	16.6	21.7	2	+2.17
15	Pervasive Software Inc	PVSW o	80	94	B	22.63	19	69	110	28	15.5	1498	+ 57	+ 62	6.6	19.7	0	+1.57
16	Broadvision Inc	BVSN o	77	97	A	72.75	9	191	983	58	25.3	5220	+300	+106	7.8	8.3	4	+2.70
17	A V T Corporation	AVTC o	93	80	C	30.63	24	29	38	9	13.1	1550	+ 43	+ 28	19.8	23.9	0	+1.53
18	Lightbridge Inc	LTBG o	75	97	A	16.50	19	55	385	15	16.1	1836	....	+ 47	− 6.9	6.3	1	+1.83
19	Microstrategy Inc Cl A	MSTR o	82	89	A	32.50	29	130	383	59	37.9	2419	+167	+ 92	9.0	3.2	5	+1.11
20	Actuate Corp	ACTU o	77	94	A	33.00	11	206	233	94	13.8	1197	....	+109	− 14.5	....	0	+2.62
21	Exchange Applications	EXAP o	77	94	B	35.00	16	250	298	104	9.8	1272	....	+ 79	− 3.5	− 6.4	9	+3.95

Business Daily or you can get these from your brokerage company as they will subscribe to various services such *Daily Graphs* that give category listings. These may be the same or very similar to those found in *IBD*.

Now you have a list from which to select one stock in this category; you want the one which is the best performer in the group. There is the simple way to do that.

I hope you haven't thrown the *IBD* paper away yet because you'll need it again. *IBD* ranks every stock according to EPS (Earning Per Share) and RS (Relative Strength). List all the stocks you can find in the *Transportation-Truck Category* down the side of a sheet of paper and then make a column for EPS and RS. Go through the stock listing until you have all those columns filled. You might see *Landair Services Inc.* (LAND) with EPS reading of 95 and RS reading of 91, *USA Truck* (USAK) with EPS 87 and RS 81, *Cannon Express* EPS 75, RS 91. Do *not* list any stock with a rating of less than 80 EPS or 70 RS. The most important number is the RS which tells you the strength of upward movement of this issue in relation to the overall market performance.

Your Weekend Graphic Review/

Every Friday you'll see "28 different graphic displays" of companies that are shown on Your Weekend Review list (a sampling displayed below). You'll probably want to keep each Friday's newspaper for further study over the weekend. Graphs show you stock symbol, (o = options), closing price & net change, shares outstanding, Industry Name, business, 3 years annual EPS Growth Rate, avg. daily volume, last two Qrts. EPS % change, Group Relative Strength (A best), PE ratio, 1 year of weekly split-adjusted prices and volume, 10 week moving average of prices, relative price strength line and number.

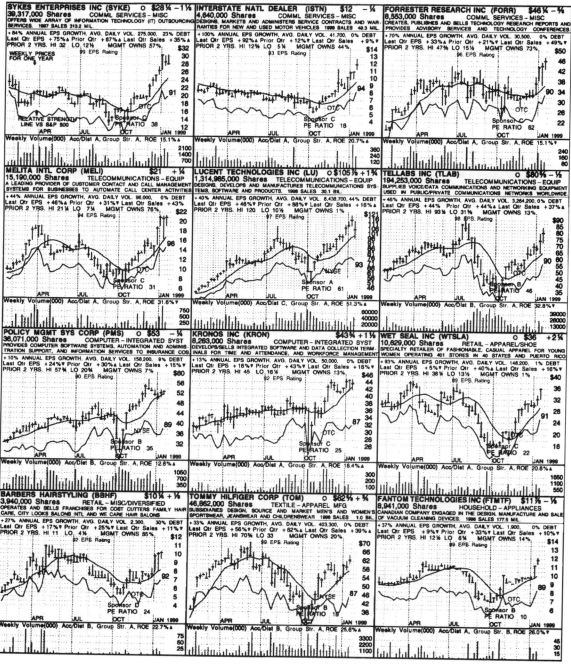

The higher the number the stronger the upward move. Anything over 80 is great, but be careful of those in the high 90's as they might be overbought. If possible take a look at the chart to confirm this upward pattern. I like to see at least a 30-degree or more upward trend. The more you come to understand what the chart is telling you, the better trader you will become. Take a look at the back page of *IBD* in the Friday edition to see 21 charts called *Your Week-end Graphic Review*. Study these. Here you may find a good candidate for a stock you want to buy.

The stocks you choose will be influenced by the stock price because you have limited funds. You should not buy something at $100 per share, as it will limit your other choices. You want to spread your money around in several issues — be diversified, as they say.

Oh yes, one more 'don't'. Don't consider any stock unless it has been listed on the exchange for one year.

You must do the same thing for each of the categories you have chosen. You now buy 100 shares of each one of those stocks for your total of about $15,000. *Don't buy them all in the same week.* Limit your purchases to one new issue each week. The reason for this is you don't know where you are in the short-term market cycle and you don't want to be buying everything just as the market is about to set back several hundred points and might drag your excellent stock with it. Immediately put in a 10% stop, GTC.

Next step. Once a week (Saturday or Sunday is good as you will have more time then, you must calculate the increase or decrease in the price from the *previous* week (not what you paid for it). This can be done in one of two ways and I will leave that up to you. Pick one and stick with it. Choose the closing price for the previous week (Friday's close) or you may take the high and low for that week and choose the mid range price. Either one will work. I like Friday's closing prices as it is easier. I said I was lazy.

When one of your stocks loses its momentum and the percentage of decrease becomes more than -7% over any two week period (and you haven't been stopped out with your 10% trailing stop), you will sell it and put those funds into your best performer, not another new issue. You now have 4 stocks. Stock A is up 4% last week, stock B is flat (no change), stock C is down 1% and stock D is up 8%. Stock E is down 9%. The money from the sale of stock E goes into stock D. When this happens to a second stock on your list you do the same thing: sell the weak and buy the strong. You are following the stocks with the greatest upward momentum. Move all stops up on Monday morning before the opening. Never move a stop down.

You now have 3 stocks that are moving up strongly. Stay with them until you are stopped out by the trailing stop. It could be several days or months. This should give you a nice profit. Start over from the top; look for 2 more stocks using the same scenario. As your funds increase you can increase your base holding to 6 stocks then 7 and so on. It is hard to keep track of more than 8 or 10 issues. As your account grows you will be able to buy 200 shares, then 300, etc. Know your limitations both financially and emotionally.

Let me explain why this very simple method works. The EPS, Earnings Per Share, is the *fundamental* reason why the stock *should* go up because it is financially strong. You know the old "shouda, wouda, couda" game. The RS, Relative Strength, will tell you how this particular stock is performing *technically* in relation to *all* other stocks on that exchange. And the Industry Prices show you which *group* is the strongest in the market today and for the past 3 months. It has been said 60% of a stock move is due to the movement of the industry group it is in, 20% is due to the quality of the company (EPS) and 20% is due to the bull or bear configuration of the entire market.

This method constantly weeds out the weak issues and keeps you in stocks that are advancing better than the overall market, not going down or sideways. You may find after a period of time that you have an *Intel* or a *Nike*. Then you can tell your friends what a great stock picker you are. It really isn't as complicated as the Wall Street types want you to think it is, but most of them can't do this simple exercise.

You will hit one, two, three or more stocks which will return 100%, 200%, 300% or more over a period of time and you risk no more than 10% of your bankroll with any position. You don't need an advisory service to do this, but I use *Pitbull* to help me find individual stocks. You can buy this method very reasonably; but it does take work. I don't claim to be smart, just smart enough to know *who* is smart so I can *follow* what *he* is doing *when* he is doing it right.

I keep telling you that stock trading is not easy and requires a lot of your attention. If you don't have the time I recommend you leave the picking of individual stocks to the professionals. Ride the coattails of the hot ones who manage mutual fund portfolios. What they neglect to tell you is they also get cold and you don't want to be with them then.

DAY TRADING

Everybody talks about day trading. It seems to have some kind of mystique. The only one who is happy with your day trading is your broker. Of course, you will be broker faster, but you will help the commission-man make another payment on his yacht.

Day trading is self-flagellation. Most people do it to see how much pain they can endure. There may be some successful day traders, but the only ones I know are professionals, so don't quit your job to do this.

When you are day trading, otherwise known as scalping, you are looking for a small edge or a quick trend that you can hop on for a few ticks and then offset the trade many times within minutes and always get out before the close of the trading session. In the old days, 10, 20 years ago, there were edges because there was a lot of customer paper to trade off. You might pick up 2 or 3 points. Today the paper is more professional and the edge has pretty much disappeared.

A friend of mine could stand in the middle of the gold pit and hear the bids and offers from different sides of the steps. They might be bidding and offering with a spread of only 1 or 2 ticks. The bid was under the offer, but they could not hear each other because of the noise. He would hit the bid and offer

of both of them and pocket the difference. A tick in gold is $10 and if he did a ten lot, he made a quick $100 or $200. He did this many times each day and always went home flat. (meaning no positions at all were carried over night).

Ray was a tall guy in the soybean pit who filled much of the customer paper and also had the ability to scalp several other markets at the same time — like orange juice, cattle and corn. He was amazing. I've never seen anyone like him.

I have stood in the corn pit and watched a scalper bid at a particular price and when there were no takers for his buy order he then offered to sell at exactly the same price. Unfortunately, when I walked into the pit they would count my money. I could never scalp successfully so I stuck to long term trading which, in commodities, was anything from overnight to longer than 2 weeks. If you were on the right side of a trade for several weeks you made a ton of money.

There are many sophisticated computer day trading software programs that may have from 5 to 30 parameters. You set each parameter yourself. The software monitors many technical price and momentum factors and spits out buy and sell recommendations. You must act immediately or not at all. These programs usually sell for about $3,000 which isn't much, if they work. The biggest flaw is the system operator — he can't pull the trigger when he gets the signal. Also almost all of them have an optimization feature which means you must fit that particular program to "current conditions" — usually meaning is the market going up, down or sideways. It is one of those "hindsight" factors. You can't know what the "current conditions" are until you look back on them and then it is too late. This applies to the same programs when applied to longer term trading.

All of the really great scalpers I have known I would call "feel" traders. They traded by the "seat-of-their-pants" method. Sometimes I would ask them what they were doing and they might say, "I don't know", yet they went home with money every day. I saw Jack walk over to the order desk with about 20 trading cards that were filled in on both sides, hand them to one of the clerks and say, "Where am I?". He knew pretty well, but he might be off one or two contracts and he wanted to be sure he had a 'buy' for every 'sell'. He may have made 20 or 30 trades for multiple contracts during the past hour.

Another friend of mine never looked at any news on the ticker before the opening bell. He would just go into the pit and start trading. I saw him make almost a million dollars one year doing this.

On Friday afternoon there were many floor traders who took off as soon as the market closed to go to Las Vegas to gamble for the weekend. They just had to have continuous action. I like the money without all the stress.

Another gentlemen I knew who owned a brokerage firm told me he could turn the market off and not think of it for the whole weekend and then come in to start trading about 20 minutes before the opening. He said it, but I still don't believe it.

Today on the Internet with electronic trading people are trying to scalp for a few ticks at home using their computers. So far I haven't met anyone who has been doing this profitably for any extended period.

For most people day trading is a death wish for their money. Of course, they won't admit it. These are the same folks who wear black clothes and ride their bikes at night on crowded highways.

If you will heed the information in this book you will not need to day trade. My method is not very exciting, but it is profitable and safe and you will sleep peacefully at night.

If you can be happy with a return of 30% to 50% or more per year then stick with the best performing mutual funds. Forget stocks.

Don't trade on margin. Yes, it will give you more leverage and it sounds good in theory, but I don't do it and do not recommend it.

It is really helpful to talk to someone about your account and trading method. That is what your broker is for, but you definitely don't want a broker. If your spouse isn't interested, see if you can find someone locally or even by long distance phone. If you each have a fax that is even better so you can send charts or magazine articles or whatever back and forth. You want to chat at least weekly and bounce ideas off each other. There are some great chat rooms on the Internet with investment-minded people. Before you join in the conversation just watch to try to find a kindred soul or ask questions like "Have you read this book?"

There are some basic rules I have made for myself over the years and I will share these with you:

1. Never trade without a stop. *7-8% drop trailing stop*

2. Never let a winning trade go to a loss.

3. Stick with your system or method.

4. Never invest in *anything* where *you* don't control the money. (Meaning you can get your money out any time you want it.)

One last bit of advice about this chapter of the book:

DON'T TRADE INDIVIDUAL STOCKS!

Options

If commodity trading is a little too fast and the leverage too much for you and the stock market is too slow and there isn't enough leverage, you might want to be adventurous and try the best of both worlds — stock options. Options have both leverage and speed.

Most people are scared away from options because the option traders speak a whole nother language. And I don't understand it either. They talk about Black/Scholes, deterioration values, betas, deltas, expiration, strike price and gosh knows what else. I probably have some of that wrong, but who cares; I just know how to make money with them. And I'll show you.

First of all, I don't think options are the least bit scary. When I put on an option position I know I can lose it all and it won't make me sick if I do. Now I have the leverage to make a big score which balances out the scare factor. Here is the reason.

My risk is limited to the purchase price. If I pay 3 ½, then I know I have $350 (plus commission) at risk for each option which represents 100 shares of stock. The stock must advance 3 ½ points for me to break even if I hold it to expiration which I don't. For 10 options, my total cash loss could be $3,500, but now I control 1,000 shares of stock. To buy 1,000 shares of stock selling for $35 per share I would have to come up with $35,000 or use margin which, at this time, is 50% so I would need only $17,500. Let's stick with the cash example. When trading I usually risk a maximum 10% stop which would be $3,500 if I bought 1,000 shares. Coincidentally, that is what I paid for my 10 options. Seems like I have the same risk. Actually less because the stock can't open through my stop and the exchange can't hurt me by suspending trading in that issue. My total risk is locked in to $3,500 plus commission.

Let's look at the leverage. Say that in 60 days the stock advances 5 points to $40 per share. My option purchase is usually in the money or as close to the money as possible and as far out as I can get at a reasonable price, usually 4 to 6 months. In this case the option was purchased at the money so I paid a premium of about 3 ½ points ($3,500) for the 180 days time I bought. Now, there will be some price deterioration during the 150 days, but by no means the full value. It usually works out to about ½ the premium (about $1750) provided you sell 30 days prior to the expiration of the option. During that last 30 days you will see the time premium go to nothing so you always want to sell at least 30 days prior to expiration whether you have a profit or not. That's my rule: sell 30 days prior to expiration, win, lose or draw. Say the option is still worth 1 ½ points for the remaining time (you paid 3 ½) plus it now has the added value of being 5 points ($5,000) in the money for a total value of $6,500. I have almost doubled my money in 60 days.

The stock went from $35,000 to $40,000 for a profit of $5,000 with a return of about 14% for the 150 days had I bought the stock instead of the option; the option returned a profit of $2,500 on a $3,500 risk investment for a return of 71% (not counting commissions in either case). Which would you rather have?

Timing is the most important thing here because your time to hold an option position is limited. Try to go 120 to 180 days out and stick to purchasing stock options close to the money or in the money where the stock price is from 20 to 60. I like to let my options run as long as possible providing the stock continues to make new highs. Many times I run a 200% or 300% profit. Sometimes I lose it all.

Here is a true story where I lost my butt, but I still consider it a positive trade because I followed all my rules. On December 21, 1998, I bought 10 Equifax, Inc. April 45 calls (symbol EFXDI) and paid $362 each plus commission. The chart looked very positive, the stock had broken out to a new 5-year high and was selling right at 45 strike price. The next day the stock was just about unchanged. The following day it was down a little more and closed at 44. Still O.K. Nothing was happening as far as I could tell. On the third day it opened at 34 — $10 lower and my options were quoted at $25. Basically worthless. Suppose I had owned the stock and had in my 10% stop. Instead of being filled at my stop price of $40.50 it would have been executed at $34 and my loss would have been an additional $6,500 to $11,000 instead of $3, 650. This why I like option trading as I know my risk is limited when I put on the trade.

Let me make it absolutely clear right here that you are NOT going to win every time, but you don't take big losses. I have found that if a stock is not moving after I buy it and have it for about 30 days then I am wrong. I sell it for a loss or a small gain, but I get out because the market is not doing what I thought it would. I don't mind being wrong for a small amount of cash, but I hate to be stupid hanging around too long for a big loss when my money could be working somewhere else. More important, you must learn to read charts well enough to be able to see strong support points (for stops) and when the stock breaks through this on a closing basis, you want to sell the option. This applies to both calls and puts. If you will learn to read charts you will definitely make more money; it will also help you to get out of a bad position. And don't pay any attention to the fundamentals as talked about by the people on CNN, your broker or any analyst. Fundamentals are great, but they won't make you money because they are not a timing tool. Usually by the time everyone knows about the true fundamentals the major part of the move is over.

I will enter 3, 4 or 5 different stocks options over a period of time and at the end of one to six weeks I will have sold out of at least half of them because they are not performing. The good calls will start going up and as they hit the next strike price I will add another position. Taking the first example above, my original $3,500 is worth $6,500. You could sell these options here, reinvest (speculate, bet, double up, whatever) and purchase twice as many new options in the same stock 120 to 180 days out. Now you have more than doubled your profit potential. This is called pyramiding. Your $6,500 could become $11,000 to $12,000. If you happen to get skillful (I'll settle for lucky) and hit one of those straight up rocket ships, you might actually end up with several hundred thousand dollars in a few months by continually rolling over and pyramiding your profits. It takes a strong stomach and cast iron discipline to do it. All you need is one of these, then put your profits in mutual funds and retire.

When doing this be careful of your tax situation if you are rolling over near the end of the year with big profits. If you have created a taxable event this year and then get hit with a big loss next year you will be in trouble. Stop the rollover once you pass into the next year unless you have nice profits which you can protect or at least get out even. You must pay the taxes on the profits you have taken this year. If you develop a loss in the next calendar year you will be limited to a portion of that amount to write off, but you can carry the loss forward if it does happen to be large. Of course, you can just keep on trading and hopefully make it up as the new year progresses. I suggest you discuss this with your accountant.

When you start getting these good hits (making big money), don't become hoggish. Stay with the nibbles. Let the position prove itself to you. Patience. You will make more money not trying to choke down the whole sandwich all at once. Bite off the little pieces and you will see how easy and delectable this method can be. You sleep better too. What I mean by this is buy one or two options and let the position make money. Don't do anything until the stock moves up to the next strike price. At that point you can double up by buying more or, better yet, you may sell the first position out for a large profit and roll the entire amount into the next strike price further out provided the stock still meets your buy requirements. It is going to take time to master this, but it is worthwhile. You will continue expanding your knowledge each day you trade. I am still learning after doing this for more than 35 years.

Here is another basic rule: *You don't tell the market what to do.* You watch and listen and you do what *it* tells you. If you are in one of those 'I hope, I hope, I hope' deals, just get out. Prayers haven't made the market go up yet.

Nowadays I only trade options, both calls and puts, but my serious money is in mutual funds. I really don't think you should be trading the dangerous stuff with the rent money. Since it is so easy to make money with a good return the average person should trade only mutual funds. It is simple and safe. Most people don't have the time or will not put forth the effort to be trading in commodities, stocks or options.

I sincerely ask you not to trade commodities, stocks or options as it takes a great deal of time and it will take you years to learn. It took me years, but maybe I'm not too bright.

Dealing only in mutual funds, you can average 30% to 50% per year over any 5-year period and that is a reasonable return. Plus you will sleep better. You know the old saw: "Bulls make money and bears make money, but hogs get slaughtered."

Reread the mutual fund chapter. Learn that. When you have extra money to throw away you can take a shot at the really high-risk equities if you want to.

DON'T TRADE OPTIONS

Commodities

This is the Formula One of trading. It is not recommended for the faint of heart or the weak of stomach. It is also the quickest way I know of to make a small fortune — provided you start with a big fortune.

There is no single book that can teach you to trade futures and I don't want you to think you are going to learn here. I will give you a few tips and some of my personal experiences which might be of help should you ever decide to throw money on these troubled waters.

There are times to trade and there are times not to trade. It is better to be standing on the sidelines with your money in your fist than sweating out an unknown. One of the hardest things for any trader is not to trade. People would come up to me on the floor and ask me what positions I had on and when I said I was flat (no positions on), they would look at me funny and ask, "How can you be down here and not trade?" Very simple. "I am not here to trade, I am here to make money." Make an embroidered doily out of that one and put in on the breakfast table. It should be your daily mantra, "I only trade to make money, I only trade to make money, I only..." Well, you get the idea.

Never hold a belly or hog position going into a Pig Crop Report. Sure, you might make a fortune, but chances are you will lose your ham. One time (only) I did stay short into a major Cattle Report (because of really strong technical factors) and I did make a small fortune, but I was young and inexperienced and I wouldn't do it today. Major reports can mean limit moves (that means it can go just so many points and then trading ceases because there is nobody willing to take the other side of the trade, like 150 points for cattle) for days. You can be locked out for days (no one will trade so you can offset your position). Don't do it.

Don't play in the distant futures options. I have seen customers take positions in silver in year-out options. I said to this guy, "Are you planning to get married to this silver? Suppose you want get out. Then what?" Forget it, few customers want good common sense advice. But if you are dumb enough to do it, let me tell you how to get out without getting killed. I had a customer with 50 silver contracts in a year out option. He had been in it for a while. Now he was trying to get out even (you've never done that). Because distant months are so thin (very small trading volume) the broker many times will take the other side of the trade for his personal account *if he wants to*. He was not about to give my customer his price. He was long so I had him put in an order to put on a bull spread at so many cents — long the nearby option and short the month he was in. We were able to do the spread which actually left him long 50 of the nearby contracts where there was plenty of action so he was able to offset without giving up any extra points. The double commission was still cheaper. Unless your broker has been around for a while, he won't know this trick. Once you tell him he will understand how it works.

NEVER trade commodities with a stockbroker. There is a world of difference in the thinking that goes into trading these two totally different kinds of financial instruments. A stockbroker just doesn't think fast enough to trade futures. He also has been taught to hold on to a losing position until it comes back where you will get out "even". He may recommend "averaging down" — another dumber. I like to call this one *Dumb and Dumber* — the broker is dumb and the customer is dumber. If you must trade commodities (and I don't recommend it), go to a house specializing in commodity futures that understands the markets and has a good technical approach, which they all do. Stick with one of the larger houses, but not the big Wall Street firms. Pick a Chicago discount company.

I remember having a sea captain for a client in the mid-70's who loved to trade pork bellies. He was long and wrong and I could not get him to place a stop. He kept sending in more money to meet his margin calls and I can't remember how many calls he answered, but it was a bunch. He was long a few contracts and now was about $12,000 in the hole. Talk about dumb! The market was still going down and he had another margin call. I said, " You must wire in the money or I will put in a stop". "No, no, don't do that. I'll send the money." But it didn't come. I told him that the house required a stop or the money. (They didn't because if he went debit the house would take it out of me and I was not about to let him get into my pocket.) I put in the stop at break even, where his account was about zero if the stop was hit. You guessed it — they got him. And the next day the market bottomed and started up. Ho boy! He told me he had to have the money back because he had taken the last $5,000 out of his wife's account and she didn't know it — yet. I think he was looking for another berth in maybe more than one way.

Another broker I worked with had a minister who had the trading habit. It was a small account, but he managed to lose $15,000. He absolutely had to have the money back and wanted to trade with no cash in his account so he could get 'even'. It seems he had 'borrowed' the money from the church account. The broker told him, "The Board giveth and the Board taketh away". The Chicago Board of Trade, that is.

Here is another basic rule: *Only trade the active options which are usually the nearby months. Never* trade in the 'spot' month — that is the current month and no longer a "future". You might get delivery and it will cost you a small fortune.

I had a potential customer who wanted to open an account with me to trade fresh eggs in the spot month. (Yes, that was a long time ago. They don't trade eggs any more because the option was very unfair to buyers who did want to take delivery.) I tried to explain to him that the contract was weighted in favor of the seller and if he got delivery he would lose an extra 5 cents per contract (about $1250/contract) because of delivery charges and reinspection. In fact, I told him he should go down to his local tattoo parlor and have engraved on his forehead in reverse script "Do not trade eggs in the spot month". That way he could see this every morning while he was shaving. I also told him I would not take his money because I knew he would lose more than he put in and go debit (which means I would probably get stuck paying it). I begged him not to do it. A few months later I called him to see what happened. There was a big sigh on the other end of the phone and he said, "Al, you were right. They killed me. I'm still paying it off". This advice goes for trading spot month in *any* commodities. Don't! That is for the pros on the floor; they will skin you alive every time.

If you trade soybeans you should always chart all the big months —

May, July and November. And watch the spread action — that is the price relationship between the nearby and distant months. This suggestion applies to all commodities. It will give you a clue as to the fundamental direction of the market.

And here is another little tidbit of information that every bean trader knows. There will never be a major bull market in soybeans (corn, wheat, oats, etc.) the next growing season unless the selling price of beans for the previous crop season was less than the cost of production. Very logical. If you were a farmer and you had a big crop last year, but the price of the beans was less than it cost you to grow them, would you be planting from fencerow to fencerow next year? Not hardly. You would be cutting back and planting another crop in hopes it would bring you some money. The actual planted acreage would shrink. Now if, at the same time, you have some world catastrophe like an El Niño or really horrendous weather for the US, South American or Chinese crops, you can then look for $10 to $12 beans. Check out the cost of production for soybeans and the selling price to see if the farmers made any money last year. See if that carryover is relatively small. Call the Chicago Board of Trade research department. They will tell you. Don't ask your broker; he probably doesn't know. Then look at the chart.

Never be short live cattle from December 15 to February 15. Almost every winter there is a major storm in the plains states and on television you see pictures of some dude kicking hay out the door of a helicopter to beleaguered starving cattle. This is usually good for one or 2 limit up days. Then you can get short if that is where you want to be. Sometimes you can sell limit up and have it good for a quick 40 to 60 points on a day trade, but you had better be an experienced trader. Don't leave this up to your broker.

Many of the soothsayers of the trading industry are wrong and can't trade their way out of a wet paper bag. See if you can get them to show you a copy of their personal trading account. I bet they won't.

When a broker, guru, seer or industry "expert" tells you that a particular commodity is below the cost of production and can't go any lower, run, don't walk, for the nearest exit. He doesn't know anything. You tell me, if you were a farmer and you had 500 acres that last year were planted to corn and beans and you lost money, do you think you would look out the door and say, "Let's not plant anything this year. We will wait for the price to go up and then we'll go back to farming again." Not hardly.

The farmer has everyone and every thing against him. He is at the mercy of the weather, the demand of the world market place, Congress with its political agenda (like the farm giveaway programs that cost taxpayers untold hundreds of millions each year), railroad strikes, foreign-grown crops, his personal health and a lot more. This also applies to every product in any industry you can think of because the owner has such a huge capital investment in land, plant and equipment that he *can't* stop production. He must continue to produce even though he may lose money on every unit.

Be a contrarian. When everyone is bullish be careful. The majority is usually wrong. They might be right for a little while, not for long.

I remember trading coffee back when it was 60 cents/pound. (Yeah. I'm that old.) Other traders were coming up to me on the floor saying, "Al, have you bought any coffee yet? It's going to the moon." My reply, "No, I'm waiting to get short". They would look horrified and ask if I was nuts. The chart was a perfect ascending triangle and had been working for about 2 or 3 months. It couldn't look much better except for one thing — the *Market Vane Bullish Sentiment Index* (this is a good technical service, but you must know how to use it) had coffee at 88% bullish. I did not want to become a lemming and go over the cliff with all the other rats. One day when the nearby option was settling on the bottom of the ascending trendline, I went short one contract on the close realizing my loss potential was only about $200. The next morning coffee opened 100 points lower smack through the trendline. The market was screaming at me. I sold 2 more contracts at the market and within 2 hours coffee was limit down. I sold one more contract before it locked. The next day it was limit down locked on the opening. The same for the following day also. I covered my position in 4 days for a $10,000 profit on just a 4 lot and I could have stayed longer, but I was happy. I took a few days off.

One of the coffee basics: Never be short May through August. That is the winter season. One good freeze can seriously hurt the crop which could send the market limit up for several days.

Coffee used to be a very thin and controlled market. I haven't traded it in so long that I don't know it any more. Back in the mid- 70's, a friend of mine was in on a coffee manipulation with Jack. Jack had spent months going back and forth to South America, getting together with certain government officials. He set up the whole operation as to the kind of news that would go out over

89

the wires and he also had a very close relationship (you know what I mean) with a gal at the major news desk in Washington who was in charge of the information that went out on a national hot line. He ran a beautiful scam. As it was nearing the top, my friend said it was time to get out because Jack was starting to believe his own press clippings. George made about $400,000. Unfortunately, I wasn't in on the deal and did not find out until it was over. At that point Jack had over $2,000,000 in paper profits. He fell in love with his own stories and did not want to sell, but still managed to get out with about $800,000.

There are very few manipulations today and almost none in U.S. commodities. The CFTC, Commodity Futures Trading Commission, and the exchanges do keep a close tab on strange movements in the markets.

My friend, George, who was in the coffee deal, was in my opinion the premier belly trader of all time. He knew the market really well. One day I heard him on the phone and when he got off I asked, "What was that you just bought?" "Oh, a carload of pigs lips." "What do you do with pigs lips?" "Make sausage out of them". You learn something new every day. This was one way of his to keep an eye on the cash market.

Another time he was short bellies in the last few days of the spot month and the market was firm. He had his margin clerk prepare 200 phony delivery notices which is quite a stack considering there weren't more than 300 deliverable belly contracts at the time. The margin clerk took them down to the floor of the exchange; he did not speak to anyone. He put them down on the company's desk on the trading floor about 20 minutes before the opening and just turned his back for about 30 seconds. Then he picked up the stack again and walked toward the exchange room. Before he even got there, the rumor ran through the floor traders that "George is delivering big numbers". The market opened close to limit down and George covered his short position. The pork belly market is wild and because of the large, violent moves is not for a novice trader or those with a heart condition.

I was a new broker working for George; everyone knew he was a stand up guy who took care of his people. When he was putting in a large order he would tell all of us in the bullpen that he was going to buy 100 bellies and he would let us frontrun him with 1 or 2 contracts. Then he would tell Jimmy in the pit to make the buy and after he got his order filled, which could run it up

10 or 20 points, he would tell us. We would sell with a nice little extra $50 or $100 for the day. At the time I did not realize that frontrunning (buying for your personal account when you know there is a large order to be executed) was illegal — and still is.

What happened? What happened in the coffee deal and in all of them like it? Very simple. The lemmings (people who were long) were following the crowd psychology and listening to everyone else who was long telling each other how smart they were. At some point the market ran out of buyers. When everyone started selling they all raced over the cliff. Once a heavily overbought market starts down it is hard to stop because even small rallies are met with sellers who are trying to get out even and others who must sell because they can't meet the margin calls. It is a cascade effect. The bullish market sentiment is one of the most important indicators you can watch. Using it with a simple trend line, you can see when the trend turns so you jump on for a fast ride either up or down.

Sometimes I have seen a trader with a losing trade who wanted to hold on to his position spread it off. He might be long July Pork Bellies with a loss of 50 or 100 points which he did not want to take. He thought the market would rally back so he would short an equal number of August Bellies against his longs, locking in the loss. Usually this is done near the close. The trader will carry the position overnight as the spread probably won't change much by the opening tomorrow. Now he thinks he has time to think about what to do, but what he really has is a balanced position with an unbalanced mind. This genius can now make two mistakes instead of one because he has to get out of both his longs and shorts by lifting one leg (option) at a time. It rarely works, as the guys who do this aren't smart enough traders to offset the longs and shorts at the right time.

I always watched the cattle when the market sentiment indicator went below 40 and bought them when they broke out over the downtrend line. Cattle are wonderful for this. I think I have made more money trading cattle like this than any option.

Another cattle tip: Key reversals in cattle do work most of the time. That doesn't mean they work all the time so you have to pay attention to your other indicators. I like to use 2 key indicators for cattle: The over-bought/over-sold index (a contrarian indicator) and a trend line. When the oversold index gets down below 40% bullish (and lower is better), put in your trend line and when it breaks up through it, buy with a stop under the low of that move. When it has been declining for a long time in commodities that may be 3 weeks to 2 months (see cattle chart below), and it is getting more and more bearish, you can usually take a position for at least a quick 200 or 300 point move. Many times I would see this happening during the day and immediately take a first position. I might add to it 2 more times during the day and frequently have the option lock limit up that day. The longer it has been going down the better chance you have for a limit up. Key reversals are common at this time and also confirm you are getting in at the right time.

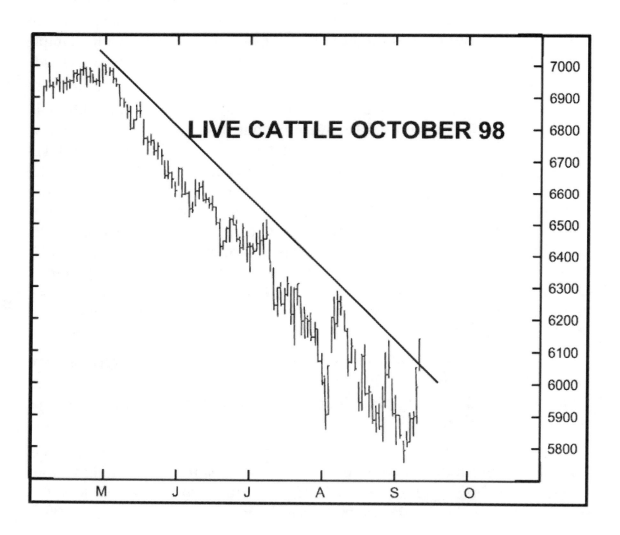

LIVE CATTLE OCTOBER 98

Copper is another one where the market sentiment will get into the high 80's. In fact, I have seen copper go to 100% bullish. The numbers are the percentage of *professional* (catch that, professional?) analysts who are watching that particular market. In my opinion they are just another one of those lemmings. These are statistics you should keep weekly and should become an integral part of your chart. There are software programs which will calculate these numbers called RSI (Relative Strength Indicators), but I always liked to know what the real people were doing so I subscribed to *Market Vane* from California. This is called contrarian trading and is not for amateurs.

I had a customer who was in the copper industry who put up $15,000 to take a long-term position for a seasonal trade. He also was buying a seasonal trading letter from one of the big names and he assured me that "Jake said" that copper goes up 8 years out of 9 from May to September (I don't remember the actual months and it isn't important). Anyway, he wanted to buy 15 contracts immediately which gave him no margin for error at that time. A 50-point move against him would have been a margin call. I said, "Why don't we do the prudent thing and scale into the position two contracts at a time as it goes up each 50 points?" Somehow, I managed to talk him into this. In the meantime, I looked at the charts, did some additional technical analysis and told him I thought this was the ninth year. Please be very careful as I didn't think it was going to work this year. "I can tell you", he said, "that copper is now below the cost of production and it can't go any lower and with this seasonal trend I'll make a fortune." Here are greed and emotional stupidity overcoming good common sense. The next day the market dropped 100 points and he insisted on buying more contracts. He wanted five. I talked him down to two. And the next day it was down another 50 and he added 2 more. "It *can't* go any lower. It's *below* the cost of production." Well, it continued to do so and he lost his $15,000 when he finally ran out of money.

The stop rule is especially valuable for people who trade in their own industry. They think they know more about their industry than anyone else. Well, let me tell you, they know even less than the average bear. Why? Because they are emotionally involved with their product and can't think logically. They always know their product is going to go up.

When I was a floor trader and had a membership for 17 years on the MidAmerica Commodity Exchange, I was on margin call many times. It means I did not have enough money in my account to carry all those positions. And I mean big calls. The margin clerk never hassled me. One day I was in his office and I asked him, " Mick, you know I have margin calls, but you never bother me like you do the other traders. How come?" He said, "Al, you always have a stop on every position." That was the old days when you could get away with not meeting calls. You can't do that any more.

I have to brag on a particular day. We used to get computer prints-outs of our positions every morning before trading started so we could check to see that they were correct. That day I had many, many sheets which showed 12 different commodity markets with multiple positions in each one and not one single losing position. I wish I had saved those pages. They should have been framed.

It wasn't always like that. Some people learn fast. I'm not one of them, I guess. When I first started trading commodities it only took me about 6 weeks to go broke. So I saved up enough over the next year or so to open another small account. This time I did not go broke for 6 months. Quite an improvement! The third time I opened an account and managed to stay even for a long time — several years. Then I began to get the hang of it and with my friends, *Patience* and *Discipline*, I began to make some serious money.

The same can happen to you. It may take time, but the rewards are there for those who have the tenacity to stick with it and use some common sense.

And, you commodity traders, take that extra money out of your trading account; it takes away your caution. You will lose it back.

When I was on the floor I had about 12 or 15 customers for years. I liked them, they liked me and they would not do dumb things — besides, I wouldn't let them. I had a six-figure income from my personal trading account so I really didn't need them for commissions. One doctor told me he had traded with every big name on LaSalle Street and I was the only broker with whom he ever made any money. We became close personal friends over the years. (Norman is gone now. I miss talking with him.)

Talk about emotions... when I was first a commodity broker, I had been talking on the phone with a man from Kentucky who was a railroad conductor and was interested in trading commodities. He said that on his next trip into Chicago he would come to my office to open an account. Sure enough, he did show up one day wearing his conductor's uniform and cap and after the usual

94

pleasantries I had him fill out new account forms. He gave the secretary a check for the munificent amount of $1,000. In those days we did not have computers, but we did have a Bunker-Ramo tote board with the prices clicking away showing the high, low and last for each option. Mr. Conductor sat down at my desk in a wooden chair with arms facing the quote board so he could watch the price changes. He decided he wanted to buy a single Live Cattle contract. In those days a 40-point move was BIG so I did not expect much — and that is what happened. Almost no action. The market was at $30.50 and after we received the confirmation of his purchase price at 30.50, he sat glued to the chair, gripping the arms, intent on each tick...30.52, 30.50, 30.47, 30.45, 30.42, 30.45, 30.47, 30.50, 30.52, 30.55 and so on for about 20 minutes. The entire range during this time was not more than 12 points; nothing happening as far as I was concerned. He was starting to get red in the face and his grip on the chair was so tight I thought he was going to pull the arms off. His knuckles were paste white. Finally he burst out, "Get me out. I can't stand the pressure". The moral of the story is, if you are a white-knuckle trader, don't get in the market.

In the late 70's I had an airline pilot who opened an account for $10,000. He would put on a position and as it went against him he would have a margin call for several thousand dollars. He always wired in more money. The market would rally and he would sell out making never more than $150. He did this 3 times and was driving me nuts because he refused to put in a stop. Each time he made a little after being in the hole big time. I wasn't sleeping nights because of his stupid trading. Finally, I sent his money back without speaking to him. He called me to ask why I had closed his account. I said, "You don't know how to trade and I refuse to have you go broke with me." "But, Al", he protested, "I've never had a losing trade." Talk about dumb. When he gets one he will have to hock his airplane.

A general does not go into battle without a plan to retreat just in case his battle plan doesn't work. The same goes for trading. Get smart! If you never learn anything else, learn to place your stops. When I had commodity customers who were trading I always insisted they put in their stops. If they didn't I wouldn't keep them as clients. I couldn't deal with those dummies and I didn't want them going broke with me as their broker.

There is a marvelous book on mass psychology, *Extraordinary and Popular Delusions of Crowds* by Charles Mackay originally published in 1841 and reprinted many times since. Every trader should read and remember it. Get it if you wish to become a serious player. The library has it.

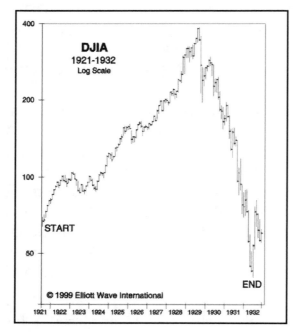

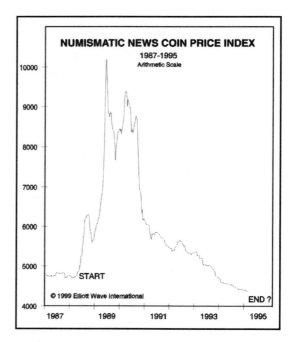

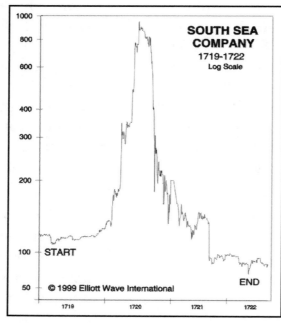

Reprinted with permission of Elliott Wave International

MARKET MADNESS
THE BEGINNING AND THE END?

There are very few services I recommend because most of them don't give good clear *simple* signals. Stay away from those complicated programs. I have been a chart reader for many years and learned the hard way. In 1960 I saw my first chart and knew that was how you trade. There is orderliness and pattern to everything in the universe; it is very clearly shown in charts if you will take the time to study them. It took me years to learn. Let's hope you are a quicker study than I was.

The old simple systems still work. You don't need $3,000 software. Over the years I've seen hundreds of trading methods and come to the conclusion that *the simple ones are the best ones*.

You must learn to take small losses. They are the keys to big profits. How many times have you heard, "Keep your losses small and let your profits run." It is true in everything you do. And here is another old saw: "The first loss is the smallest loss." Only about 40% of my trades were profitable in commodities, but half of those were very large profits. The basic key to all trading is to limit your losses; you want to win $3.00 or $4.00 to every dollar you lose. Even in stock trading, I am only right half the time.

Chart patterns work out about 70% to 80% of the time. That is why you should learn to recognize basic patterns. If nothing else, they will keep you out of a bad position. When in doubt stay out or get out.

Now that I think about it I have never known any school teacher who was a successful commodity trader (for example, an economics professor I knew blew away $80,000 in 6 months because he knew the cattle fundamentals, but didn't know squat about technical analysis). Hey, school teachers, don't get mad, get smart! Learn what I tell you in this book.

When you finish out a trade don't look back. In other words take that chart out of your book for a couple of weeks. You don't want to look at it because you will be tempted to buy back in for more of the move. Now you have the additional burden of emotion clouding your mind. You are not thinking logically. Just like my broker who made $150,000 and gave it back and more the next month. He was short and fell in love with the short side. That is another reason to take that vacation when you make a big hit.

Using my method, most commodity groups aren't worth trading more than once or twice a year.

When the bullish percentages in cattle run 80% or more for 3 weeks in a row you can mortgage the farm and be short because it is always good for a sharp break of several hundred points. Have your sell stops waiting under that trendline.

Even if you are not a "chartist", you must keep charts just to see where the main support and resistant areas are. Even the fundamentalists do.

If the same commodity is traded on more than one exchange have your orders executed on the exchange where there is the most volume and open interest. Do not trade thin commodities, options or stocks. That means there must be good volume so you can get decent execution when you want to get out. I don't care how good-looking the chart is or if the fundamentals are great. Pass.

And never take a "tip" on either stocks or commodities. If it has gotten all the way down to you, I can guarantee just about everyone else in the world knows it too. Pass.

Every growing season they lose the crop three times. In the spring, you get a rally because it is too wet or too dry. In the summer it rallies because it is too wet or too dry. And in the fall, you get a rally because they can't get the machinery into the fields to harvest because it is too wet. Then they bring in a bumper crop.

Watch the news. That old saw is still true. "Buy the rumor, sell the news." In 1998 we had coffee run up over $3.00 on all kinds of rumors that they were going to lose the crop. Then with no news (they could not confirm the crop loss) it dropped almost a dollar – that's about $35,000 per contract.

If news is bullish and it doesn't put the market up, something is going on. You don't have to know what it is as it really doesn't make any difference. Move your stops up or start looking for a place to get short. If the news is negative and the prices advance, this is really bullish. Get in or add to your position. It has a lot higher to go.

Remember this one? *Prior to* the Iran/Iraq sinking of freighters in the Persian Gulf in May-June 1984 crude oil futures advanced about 100 points, but *when* the ships were being sunk, the market started down. That news should have put crude prices up substantially. It didn't indicating lower prices to come.

A Pig Crop Report can move a market limit for 3 days; however, if the market opens 100 points higher and goes limit up but can't hold limit, you can take a shot and go home short. You should have a lower opening next day. Don't forget your stop.

A bullish report with a lower close is very bearish.

It is not my intention to teach you how to trade futures. In fact, I want you to understand how difficult and risky it is. If you need excitement in your life try to find something where you will just break a few bones, not lose your money. How about sky diving or bungee jumping? They are much safer.

My final thoughts. It requires a great deal of time and effort, a computer with real time quotes, some good software and years of practice. I am too laid back any more for this; besides, I make a nice income from my mutual funds working less than one hour each month.

DON'T TRADE COMMODITIES

6

Bonds

I guess I will have to put in a little something about bonds because if I don't, you will be asking why I left it out. In a nutshell, don't buy bonds or bond mutual funds.

Here's why:

It is very rare you will ever make any money or have a decent income from bonds. The average return is about 5% to 7% which won't even buy you cat food.

Before you we go any further, I can hear you shouting about the safety of bonds. Well, almost. Remember the Whoops bonds from a Washington state utility that went belly up? I had money in an oil venture that bought bank CDs (Certificates of Deposit, that's a bank bond). The money was parked there while the deal was being finalized, but the bank went under and we lost it all. Sure, bonds may have a place, but not for me and also not for you if you want to make any serious money.

The method I recommend in this book is, in my opinion, just as safe as bonds and will make you 10 times more money.

Every Wall Street professional loser recommends that you buy bonds when you retire and I say that is grossly stupid. Just keep doing what is recommended here and forget bonds. Keep on making 30% and 40% or more year in and year out. You can take a lot more money out and have a much nicer life style for your retirement than you ever will with bonds.

As I have said I don't trade on margin, but I do have a margin account. When I need funds I call the brokerage house and tell them to send me a check — $2,000, $3,000, $5,000 — whatever I want. It goes out the next day. If I am fully invested (as I usually am), they "loan" me the money from the margin account and charge me interest at the broker loan rate which is about the cheapest interest rate there is. The next time I have a sell signal or a switch signal from one mutual fund to another I pay off the "loan" amount. For example, if you were drawing out $2,000 each month for 5 months you would owe the broker $10,000 plus a small amount of interest. Then you had a switch signal on one of your mutual funds so you sold it for $45,000. Of the $45,000 proceeds, you paid off the $10,000 that had been advanced by the broker and reinvested the remaining $35,000 in another mutual fund. It's that simple.

When you have a "Sell" signal and you are out of the market you can be in a money market fund composed of short-term government bonds. The rate of return will fluctuate, but so what — you are only waiting for the next "Buy" signal. There will be interest income so it won't be a total loss and you will not be losing your precious capital while the market is going down. This particular type of money market fund will not flucuate in value as many other bond funds do. Most all fund families have these and almost all discount brokerage houses have them also. Ask for them. There is no commission for these so you may immediately transfer the funds back to your selection of mutual funds when you have the new "Buy" signal. A broker will try to have you buy some kind of "safe" bond on which he gets a nice commission and when you read the fine print you might even see an additional penalty should you decide to sell them back sooner than the broker wants you to.

Long term bonds like *Ginny Maes* and *Zero Coupons* are chancy because the face amount of the fund (the amount you invested) will vary from day to day depending upon the change of interest rates. If interest rates go up, you will get back less principal (money you put in) when you sell them. Unless you understand interest rates, you will NOT want to invest in this type of security.

If you understand this program you will never buy bonds.

DON'T BUY BONDS

7

The Bear

I finished writing most of this book about the first of July 1998; my mutual fund portfolio has been 100% long since January of 1995. On Friday July 24, 1998 the *Pitbull Crash Index* gave a sell signal. It confirmed many of the very weak technical indicators I watch and Maverick Investing was very close to a 'Sell' signal.

I look at a lot of stuff you will never have to see and saw the technical degradation of the whole market. I did not wait for a confirming signal from *Maverick Investing* (which you should do) and sold all my stock positions on July 27 (Dow 30 closed at 9028 and July 28 the Dow 30 closed at 8934). On July 27 I also bought some *Rydex Ursa* (RYURX), the fund that is always short the *S&P500*, and awaited the confirming signal from *Maverick Investing*. It gave a sell signal on August 11 and on August 12 I added additional positions in *Rydex Ursa* and *Prudent Bear* (BEARX). This is the most difficult time of your long-term investment program as everyone will be telling you that this is just a correction in the market and not to sell, especially the mutual fund and stock "experts". These are the "experts" who told you not to sell in October of 1987. The same when you have been out of the market sitting on cash; then all the seers will be telling you that the market is going even lower. Just follow the signals mentioned here as they come and you will be money ahead.

Once in a great while there will be a whipsaw. At these happenings you may lose a few percentage points. The worst that *Maverick Investing* has ever lost as a result of one of their signals was about 6%. It does happen, but very seldom and then for a minor amount. This is where your mettle to follow the discipline of this method will be tested. Every sense you have will be shrilling that you are doing the wrong thing. Tough it out and do it. You will never have a 20%, 30% or 40% loss like the 'Buy and Hold' crowd.

As an airplane pilot, I will tell you that when you are flying in marginal or poor weather, your senses will fool you that you are going up or going down when you are not; however, you must keep your eyes on the instruments and do exactly what they tell you to maintain a steady course. Never mind all those other messages from your senses. They are wrong just as almost all the "experts" in the financial community are wrong both at the top and bottom of the market. Follow the signals; follow your instruments. They are right; your "gut feeling" is wrong.

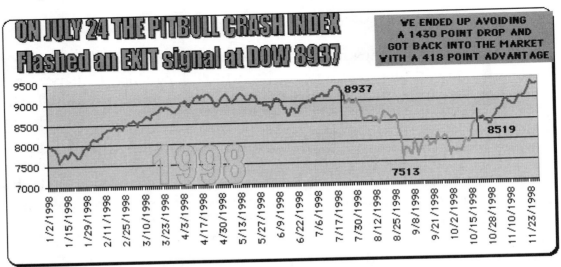

Most people were wringing their hands in August and September of 1998. I was both in cash and short, waiting for my next "Buy" signal.

It came from *Maverick Investing* on November 4, 1998 and the next day I turned around and went long in 100% of my portfolio. I had covered all short positions. For the entire year of 1998 I had eleven offsets, all profitable, and by the end of the year I had a profit of 40% not counting any profit I would have made on the money I took out for my living expenses, travel, etc. It would not have come to 50%, but definitely several points more. Fifty percent is always my target for the year. See the exhibits of all the trades and the verification letter from my CPA.

Please read this book several times. Once is not enough because you have been given such an overwhelmingly bad diet of so-called "investment advice" over the years that it will take several readings and a good deal of mental purging on your part to "unlearn" those old beliefs. If you belong to an investment club please share the book with everyone there so they can begin to think for themselves. If not, do yourself a favor and drop out.

This book is written for people with small amounts of money — those who have less than $50,000 in retirement accounts and who want to make a good return on their money with maximum safety. By following this advice you will never experience a major drawdown in your account and you will maximize your investment return. If you have ever gone through a major bear market (and most of the children managing mutual funds today haven't), you know the sickening feeling of watching your money evaporate right in front of your eyes. You older folks know what I mean. You must stop listening to the Wall Street professional losers.

Everyone, young and old, must protect his money from the swings of the market and the terrible advice of brokers and other "experts". Take charge of your own destiny. Do not rely on others when you can do a better job for yourself.

I am not an "expert" even though I have been trading for more than 35 years. I remain a student and am always looking for ways to improve my performance with simple, non-esoteric, no-nonsense methods.

If you have something you think I should know please send an email to al@mutualfundmagic.com and maybe I'll include it in subsequent revisions of this book.

Always remember...

IF IT DOESN'T GO UP, DON'T BUY IT!

by Charles Petersen

Never, Never Land

Over the years I have seen people do things with their money that are almost unbelievable. At the time they thought it was a good idea, but most of them ended up costing substantial amounts. For the heck of it let's take a look. I'm sure you know all the rules and wouldn't violate any of them. Maybe you will want to put a light pencil mark next to some. Very light, so you can erase it and no one will ever know.

1. *Never borrow to invest in the market.*

2. *Never trade without a stop-loss order.*

3. *Never take advice from a broker.*

4. *Never take a tip from a friend.*

5. *Never let a winning trade go to a loss.*

6. *Never try to pick bottoms — or tops.*

7. *Never buy a stock or fund that is in a downtrend.*

8. *Never trade on margin.*

9. *Never invest in anything where you don't control the money.*

10. *Never day trade.*

11. *Never buy a stock because "it can't go any lower".*

12. *Never buy a mutual fund until it has a one-year track record.*

13. *Never cheat on your taxes.*

14. *Never pay more tax than you have to.*

15. *Never believe the old saw that you must have a million dollars to retire.*

16. *Never stop watching your financial advisor's performance.*

17. *Never allow your financial advisor to withdraw money from your account for any reason.*

18. *Never listen to an economist.*

19. *Never invest in any thinly traded equity.*

20. *Never buy a limited partnership.*

And I know there are many more.

9

My Favorite Sources

Fabian Maverick Advisor

A major simple timing device; you need this unless you are willing to create your own index and keep up with the *Pitbull Crash Index*. May be used in conjunction with each other. I watch both. Their most important service is they get you out of the market during major down drafts to preserve your capital. Losing money is very hard on your physical and emotional health. Send for their real-time track record.

Fabian Maverick Advisor
(formerly Fabian Investment Resource)
Box 2538
Huntington Beach, CA 92647
(800) 950-8765.
http://www.fabian.com

NoLoad Fund*X

When *Maverick Advisor* says "BUY" you will need this service. They have been tracking many of the best performing mutual funds since 1976, but they also have left out some of the new better performing funds and still keep some dogs on the list. I disagree with their philosophy of being in the market at all times; they have their reasons as I mentioned in the text. Keep in mind everyone has an axe to grind. You need to know where *they* are coming from so you won't get *your* head chopped off.

DAL Investment Company
235 Montgomery St., #662
San Francisco, CA 94104
(800) 763-8639
http://www.fundx.com

Discount Brokers

I switched my account from Schwab and no longer recommend them because they require you to hold your fund for 180 days or they charge ½% to ¾% commission. Too rich for me. Fidelity also charges commissions.

Accutrade	www.accutrade.com
Datek	www.datek.com
Discover Brokerage	www.dbdirect.com
DLJ Direct	www.dljdirect.om
E*Trade	www.etrade.com
Quick & Riley	www.quickwaynet.com
Suretrade	www.suretrade.com
Waterhouse Securities	www.waterhouse.com

There are too many discount brokerage companies to mention them all here and their rules for no transaction fee trading vary considerably. Be sure you check each one yourself as they change. Look in Investor's Business Daily, the Wall Street Journal, CNBC-TV or almost any financial publication and you will see advertisements. They all perform about the same service, but some have excellent proprietary web sites and some have local offices. See which one best fits your needs. Stay away from so-called "full service" brokers which means they will charge you exorbitant commissions and will give you "advice" which you definitely don't want.

Wellington Financial Newsletter

I have known Bert Dohmen for more than 25 years and think his overall assessment of national and world markets and economics will give you a realistic perspective of what and why events are occurring. He is a good trader, but his method is different than I have outlined here. This is an optional publication and can be purchased later on as you have the extra income to justify it. Send for a sample copy.

Dohmen Capital Research Institute, Inc.
1132 Bishop Street, Suite 1500
Honolulu, HI 96813
(800) 992-9989
email: dohmcap@aol.com
http://www.dohmencapital.com

Pitbull Investor

The best and simplest stock trading method I have ever seen which you can do without a computer. W. Henry Ford, the owner and founder of this method, has more market understanding in his little finger than most of the Wall Street talking heads put together. The key is simplicity using a combination of technical indicators that are based on fundamentals. The KISS formula. You might want to buy just his Pitbull Crash Index formula and do it every day. I do. Takes about 60 seconds. You may use this indicator, but it is not necessary in conjunction with Investment Resource for your "Buy" and "Sell" signals. The PCI is much more sensitive than the IR and will give more buy and sell signals. PCI will almost always be ahead of the IR signal.

IMF Corporation
27068 La Paz Road, #501
Laguna Hills, CA 92656
(800) 491-9951
http://www.wwfn.com

Investor's Business Daily

You can subscribe or just buy the Monday edition that comes out on Saturday and has Friday's closing prices. Did you follow that? They currently have a free 2-week trial subscription. I like this paper better than the Wall Street Journal because it is more technically oriented.

Call 800-306-9744

It has taken me 30 years to distill this list to the above publications. There may be others just as helpful, but I am not aware of them. These work for me. That's my disclaimer. If you like what I have told you then do it. It works. If not, take the book back.

All of the above cost money, but they are worth every cent in my opinion. I can't say that about most of the junk that is being peddled. Get a sample issue or information to see if you like it. Free is the right price.

My email address is **al@mutualfundmagic.com** All comments are appreciated. I'll try to reply if I have the time or I'm not out fishing. After all, fishing is not a matter of life and death, it is more important than that.

Now you go catch a big one.

Al

Glossary

Accumulation

A stock remains within a price range of about 10% of its selling price for a long period of time that could be from several weeks to many months. If it breaks out to the upside the experts will tell you there has been a long period of Accumulation; however, if it breaks out to the downside the same experts will tell you there has been a period of Distribution. The experts don't know. Don't listen to them.

Annual Report

A report usually made by a CPA firm that tells you what the company has been doing with your money. Shows annual sales, balance sheets, operating statements, earnings (if any) and lots of complicated footnotes that very few people understand. The footnotes are where they hide all the stuff they don't want you to know. Most of these numbers reflect what went on over a whole year and are therefore distorted by the time pattern. Basically worthless. It would be useful if you want to buy their business or loan them money, but has no bearing on which way the stock price is headed.

Ask

The lowest price at which an investor is willing to sell — stocks, bonds, options, commodities or anything else for that matter.

Basis

The price that you paid for the shares including all fees and commissions. Mainly for tax purposes.

Basis Point

The smallest measure for quoting yields on bonds; one basis point is .01 percent of the yield of the bond. Also used to quote interest rates. One hundred basis points is equal to one percent, 50 basis points is equal to ½ percent.

Bear Market

Any time the stock market as a whole as measured by the Dow Jones Industrial Average or the Standard & Poor's 500 Index loses 20% or more of its value. You don't want to be in the market during these times.

Beta

A measure of volatility.

Black-Scholes Theory

Mathematical equations used to determine the valuation of options. Too complicated for my head. If they really worked all option traders would be rich.

Bid

The highest price a buyer is willing to pay to purchase a security.

Blue Chip Stock

This is supposed to be the highest quality stock on the market, but you can still lose money with them. This is more of the smoke and mirrors mystique. There is only one type of "blue chip" stock and that is the one that goes up after you buy it. All the rest are dogs.

The historical derivation goes back to the old, old days when you played poker and the most expensive chips on the tables were blue.

Bond

A certificate which sets forth the amount of money you have lent a company or the government along with the terms and conditions of repayment.

Book Value

The total of all the company's assets less the intangible assets and liabilities such as bonds. The final figure might be more or less than the market value of the company.

Broker

One who makes you broker. Especially if you take his advice. Remember, he works on commission.

BS

Brilliant Strategy. Barbra Streisand. Brown Stuff. Whatever. Words of "advice" from your broker or financial planner.

Buy Price

The price paid for the shares when purchased. If you paid 40½ for 100 shares it adds up to $4,050. Of course you are going to have to add on the commission and fees that might come to several hundred dollars more depending upon the brokerage house. Discount brokers' commissions are much lower so if you learn how to trade on the Internet, it will be even lower.

Call

Call option. The right to purchase a certain company's shares at a certain fixed price some time in the future no matter what the price of that security is at that time. You need not exercise this right should the security value be less and you may sell it any time prior to the expiration date.

CD Certificate of Deposit

A debt instrument usually issued for a period of less than 5 years that pays interest only and the full sum at maturity. This is not what you want if you are building toward a retirement account. Many times it will not keep up with the rate of inflation.

Closed-end Mutual Fund

This type of fund sells only a fixed number of shares. The fund is then traded like a stock. It is listed in the stock section of the newspaper, not with the mutual funds. Most of these funds sell at a discount to the sum total of the shares. It is rare to see them sell at full value, but once in a while they may even sell at a premium. I don't recommend them.

Commission

The vig. The juice. What the broker extracts from you for performing the service of purchasing and registering the stocks you purchase in your name. The less you pay the better for you.

Commodity Future

The right to purchase at today's price a particular food item, metal or financial instrument to be delivered to you according to contract specifications at some specific time and place in the future. It might be wheat, pork bellies (that's uncured bacon), gold, treasury bills, oil, lumber, stock indexes, foreign currencies, etc. This is not where you want to put you retirement funds. For pros only or those who have more money than brains.

Correction

Another Wall Street euphemism for the market going down the sewer. A downward move of less than 20% (that's a bear). If you are concerned and call your broker he will always tell you this is a correction and the market will come back. Right? Many corrections are in the 10 to 15% category. When the market is at Dow 10,000, it means the market can drop more than 1,000 points and still be in an up trend. Follow the signals in this book and you will sleep peacefully at night.

Derivative

When a security is split into its parts and each part then sold as a separate item. A zero coupon bond stripped of the dividends and is sold at a discount representing the time value of the bond to maturity. Derivatives are more dangerous than commodity futures; the leverage is sometimes 100 times the price paid. Stay away. You can become bankrupt with these.

Distribution

Opposite of accumulation. See above. This is the wild part of the market and many times distribution will be in a 20% trading range for several months before it tanks.

Dividend

An amount paid to a shareholder of the company stock that represents a distribution of part of the profits of the company. I don't pay any attention to dividends as I am more interested in price appreciation. Many company stocks go up that have never paid any dividends. An overrated reason to buy a stock.

DJIA Dow Jones Industrial Average

Also called the Dow, the Dow 30. Comprised of 30 large company stocks trading on the New York Stock Exchange and is the best known of all U.S. indexes. There are hundreds of indexes not just for stocks, but for everything including, bonds, currencies, commodities and on and on. Each foreign exchange has several. I like the S&P 500 better. See S&P.

Dumb

Advice from a broker.

Dumber
Anyone who takes advice from a broker.

Economist
One who knows all about everything in the local, national and world economies, but knows nothing about how to apply it to practical situations. The last one to ever consult for investments.

EPS Earnings Per Share
The total of company profits divided by the number of shares. Each day in the *Investor's Business Daily* newspaper you will find this figure in the stock listings as a ranking of where the stock stands in relation to all other stocks on that exchange. You don't want to own any stock with a rating of less than 80. Also note that just because it may have a high rating does not guarantee it is going to go up. See RS, relative strength as a companion to EPS.

Exchange
Where securities orders of listed companies are matched with buyer and seller. The big exchanges are the New York Stock Exchange (NYSE) and the National Association of Securities Dealers (NASDQ). Both are usually quoted on the nightly news. Unlisted securities are sold Over The Counter (OTC) by your broker by certain brokerage houses that 'make the market' in that particular issue. Transfer of ownership need not be done through an exchange; you may sell the stock certificate to another person by merely endorsing the certificate on the back.

Fed Funds Rate
Actually Federal Funds Rates are set by the Federal Reserve Board. The amount of interest charged by one bank to another bank when it loans money on overnight transactions. This is the Feds way of trying to micromanage the economy.

Float
Many times referred to as the total number of shares outstanding and available for trading. Actually most shares are squirreled away and not traded. The true float is a certain percentage of the outstanding shares that are actively traded. This number will vary widely from issue to issue. Usually the smaller the float, the more violent the price action and wider the spread.

High

The highest price that a security, stock or option sells at during a specific time frame such hour, day, week, month, year or longer.

Hypothetical

This is another term for smoke and mirrors. You will receive advertising for a system some highbinder is trying to sell you with a table of big profits from trading his method. In fact, it has a money back guarantee, but not on what you lost using it. At the bottom is an asterisk * with very fine print that tells you the results are fictitious. Trash it.

Insiders

The officers and directors of the company or anyone who owns more than 10% of the outstanding stock which means he has "inside" information that may be used for trading purposes. For listed securities these people are required to report their purchases and sales to the Securities and Exchange Commission that publishes them in a special bulletin that you may order at no charge. There are several advisory services that compile these numbers with comments. Another technical tool. If I were an "insider" I'd have an account in my wife's name at a Swiss brokerage house. I'm sure glad those folks are so honest and report everything.

IPO Initial Public Offering

Stock being offered for the first time to the public with the issuance of a prospectus. And lots of hype by the selling broker. You know what I have to say about both of these in the preceding pages. Nothing positive.

KISS

Keep It Simple Stupid. The best trading systems, whether mathematical, psychological or technical, follow this method. The more complicated the method the less likely it is to work.

LEAP

A long term option usually going out more than one year

Load - No-Load

Commission. Many times as high as 8½%. If you buy $10,000 worth of a load fund with 8½% commission you pay $850 to the broker. You now have $9,150 invested. Most people figure the market has to go up 8.5% to get "even". Wrong.

It actually takes more than a 9.25% increase to get you almost even. I don't like starting this deep in a hole. Don't buy load funds; there are too many good no-load funds that do not charge any commission. There are also many low-load funds; I don't even buy these. Some funds such as Fidelity charge a one time low-load commission and then allow you to switch from fund to fund within the Fidelity group at no commission charge. There is no correlation showing that a commission fund performs better than a no-load fund. Your broker will tell you this but he is lying.

Long
The buyers, owners of the security.

Low
The lowest price that a security, stock or option sell for during a specific time such as minute, day, month, year, etc.

Margin
A brokerage company will lend money at their broker loan rate to purchase additional shares using a certain percent of the value of your stocks. Currently it is 50%. If you have $100,000 in marketable securities in your account you may purchase up to $50,000 of additional shares in the same or other companies. I don't recommend this. Also a margin account gives your brokerage company the right to loan your securities to people who are selling short.

Market Value of the Company
Also Market Cap or Market Capitalization. The price of the shares times the number of outstanding shares of the company. Pretty much a meaningless figure, but the "experts" all talk about it. I can't see how knowing this will ever make you any money.

Money Market
A fund composed of short-term interest bearing government bonds, T-Bills or commercial paper. A good, safe place to park your money during a bear market.

Moving Average
The sum of a number computed by adding up all the closing prices of the stock, bond or mutual fund for a period of time, such as 200 days, and then dividing by 200 to give you the 200-day moving average which is plotted daily to form a line on a chart. Any time period may be used such as 10 days, 50 days, etc. When

two moving averages with different periods of time are used to create lines that cross this is called an oscillator.

Municipal Bond
A bond issued by a state or local government usually, but not necessarily for, a specific project. Many, not all, are tax exempt.

Mushroom
Something kept in the dark and fed brown stuff. Customer.

Mutual Fund
A company organized under the rules and regulations of the Securities and Exchange Commission that collects money from various individuals, companies or other entities in order to invest in stocks, bonds and/or other types of securities. The share price of an open-end mutual fund will change daily as to the total net asset value divided by the number of shares outstanding.

Net Asset Value
In the paper it is listed as NAV. The total value of all assets in a mutual fund cash, stocks, bonds — divided by the total number of shares outstanding.

Oscillator
The use of two or more differently computed moving averages to create crossover patterns that give buy and sell signals.

P/E Price/Earnings Ratio
The price of the stock divided by the earnings of the stock. This can be over any period of time even a future projection, but usually refers to the past year. If a stock is selling for $100 and has earned $10 for the past year it has a P/E of 10. Many stocks have P/E's of 30, 40, 50 or more which makes them more "speculative". The higher the P/E the riskier the stock is considered.

PUT
Put option. The opposite of a call option. The right to sell a fixed number of shares of a certain security at some time in the future at a designated price. You may or may not own the stock when the put is issued.

RS Relative Strength
A number that describes the comparative strength of a particular stock to other stocks. *Investor's Business Daily* newspaper publishes a number that identifies

a particular stock in relation to all other stocks on that exchange. You should not own a stock with an RS of less than 70. For example, a stock with a rank of 83 means it has a stronger upward price movement than 83% of all other stocks. Do you want to own a stock with a rating of 40, 33, 17 or any number less than 70? Any stock with a rating of less than 70 is a dog.

Shares

Securities that represent equity ownership. Most of them traded on the major exchanges are common shares. The fancier the name the more complicated the instrument.

Short

You sell what you don't own by borrowing the security from someone you don't know at the brokerage house to sell to another person you don't know because you think the price will go down so you can pay the guy you don't know who you borrowed the stock from. You have looked into the future and said I want to buy this $40 stock at a lower price so I'll sell it today and buy it when it goes down to $30 or whatever. Let me warn you. If it keeps going up you can be in deep do-do. This is one time you better have a buy stop in place. Markets go down about three times faster than they go up. I like the short side, but it is not for everyone.

S & P Standard & Poor's 500

This index is composed of 500 different stocks traded on the New York Stock Exchange, but it is weighted by the size of the company. That is claimed by the "experts" to be a drawback to its accuracy. However, its following is quoted almost as much as the *Dow 30*. These same "experts" say it is poorly weighted so it is a poor indicator and should not be used as a gauge of their mutual fund performance. Yet they are the first ones to shout from the top of the Empire State building that they beat the S&P500. Hey, guys, you can't have it both ways.

Social Security Trust Fund

There ain't no such thing. This is 'Washingtonspeak' for your taxes going into the general fund that the politicians spend any way they want to. It is merely a governmental Ponzi scheme and will die of its own weight or be cut back severely some time in the future.

Spread

The difference between the bid and asked prices of a stock, option or other security. I have seen so-called spreads advocated in stock trading, but not with my money.

In commodities you may buy or sell a near option and buy or sell the distant option having two positions, long one and short the other. Money is made or lost as the spread widens or narrows depending on your position and market fundamentals.

Stop

There are both sell stops and buy stops. If you own a stock and wish to limit your loss to a specific amount, or to exit your position should the stock take an unexpected tumble, you may place an order with the broker to sell when the stock trades at a specified price. For example you bought a stock at $28 and it is now trading at $44. You may place a GTC Stop at $40. GTC means Good Until Cancelled and also called an Open Order. If the stock trades at or below the $40 price, you will be filled at the next trade price. You are not guaranteed the $40 price. Should the market open sharply lower the next day you will be filled in the opening range even if it might be at $30. I have had it happen to me. If you feel you have been ripped off you may request a "Time & Sales Report" from your broker which shows every trade and the time the trade was executed along with the time your order was entered and the time it took to get to the floor. Sometimes an adjustment will be made.

Strike Price

The price agreed upon in the call or put. If a stock is selling at $25/share, you might purchase a call with a strike price of $25, say 90 days in the future. You think the stock price is going to advance over the next 60 days and you wish to be able to purchase shares at that time at the $25 price. $25 is the strike price. Of course, you will pay a premium for this privilege, but if the stock advances substantially it should be a very profitable trade.

Symbol

The letters used to designate a particular security. In mutual funds the symbol for *Rydex Ursa Fund* is RYURX, for *General Motors* it is GM.

Volume

The number of shares or contracts traded between buyer and seller during any period of time designated.

Valuation

Valuation is in the mind of the beholder. Various experts who write market advisory letters and investment columns for brokerage houses have some weird way of figuring that some stocks are undervalued or overvalued. One 'expert' will say a stock is *undervalued* and another *expert* at a different brokerage house will tell you that same stock is *overvalued*. The value of a stock is what it sells for that day even though tomorrow the same issue may be selling for more or less. Part of the Greater Fool Theory.

Volatility

The wild gyrations of price either in the general market or individual issues. As we used to say, "There's blood in the pit today".

Volume

The number of shares traded during a specific time period — minute, hour, day month, year or longer.

Zero Coupon Bond

A debt instrument that pays no interest. It is sold at a discount price that depends upon the time to maturity and the rate of interest quoted.

FINIS

ACTUAL PERFORMANCE 1998

FUND NAME	SYMBOL	BUY DATE	PRICE	SELL DATE	PRICE*	PROFIT/ LOSS	%	MO. HELD
Invesco Strategic FinanciAL	FSFSX	6/17/97	$27.12	7/27/98	$38.04	$10.92	9%	13
Safeco Growth	SAFGX	11/11/97	$24.62	6/1/98	$29.67	$5.05	30%	7
Oakmark Select	OAKLX	12/2/97	$16.43	5/5/98	$19.58	$3.15	9%	5
American Century Equity Growth	BEQEX	12/4/97	$21.45	7/13/98	$26.22	$4.77	35%	8
American Century Equity Income	TWEIX	12/8/97	$7.82	3/9/98	$8.30	$0.48	33%	4
Montgomery Global Community	MNGCX	3/8/98	$19.73	7/28/98	$24.07	$4.34	11%	4
Scudder Greater European Growth	SCGEX	5/11/98	$27.47	7/28/98	$28.94	$1.47	5%	3
Janus Twenty	JAVLX	7/13/98	$44.82	7/27/98	$45.08	$0.26	11%	1
Rydex Ursa	RYURX	7/27/98	$9.40	All Shares Sold on 10/19/98				
Rydex Ursa	RYURX	8/12/98	$10.24	10/19/98	$10.35	$0.38	21%	2
Prudent Bear	BEARX	8/12/98	$5.99	10/19/98	$7.18	$1.19	20%	2
American Century 2020	BTTTX	6/9/98	$32.68	All Shares Sold on 10/13/98				
American Century 2020	BTTTX	8/11/98	$34.29	All Shares Sold on 10/13/98				
American Century 2020	BTTTX	8/21/98	$34.29	All Shares Sold on 10/13/98				
American Century 2020	BTTTX	8/31/98	$35.70	10/13/98	$34.66	$1.04	3%	3

*includes capital gains and dividends reinvested
*11 offsets, all profitable

Invesco Strategic Utilities	FSTUX	11/5/98	$15.11	Position Held as of December 31, 1998
Reynolds Blue Chip Growth	RBCGX	11/5/98	$40.52	Position Held as of December 31, 1998
Invesco Strategic Health	FHLSX	11/9/98	$63.16	Position Held as of December 31, 1998
Janus Twenty	JAVLX	11/9/98	$44.11	Position Held as of December 31, 1998

ACTUAL PERFORMANCE 1999

FUND NAME	SYMBOL	BUY DATE	PRICE	SELL DATE	PRICE*	PROFIT/ LOSS	%	MO. HELD
Invesco Strategic Utilities	FSTUS	11/5/98	$15.11	2/9/99	$16.24	$1.13	9%	3
Reynolds Blue Chip Growth	RBCGX	11/5/98	$40.52	6/18/99	$53.52	$13.00	30%	8
Invesco Strategic Health	FHLSX	11/9/99	$63.16	2/10/99	$68.50	$5.34	9%	3
Janus 20	JAVLX	11/9/98	$44.11	6/07/99	$61.70	$17.59	35%	8
RS Information Age	RSIFX	2/12/99	$19.23	9/22/99	$26.61	$7.38	33%	7
Rydex OTC	RYOCX	2/12/99	$44.39	8/12/99	$49.89	$5.50	11%	6
Pro Fund Ultra OTC	UOPIX	2/22/99	$135.63	4/19/99	$127.87	($7.76)	(5%)	2
Trans American Premium Small Cap	TPSCX	2/22/99	$21/12	4/9/99	$23/86	$2/74	11%	2
Strong Blue Chip 100	SBCHX	4/9/99	$18.33	6/8/99	$16.53	($1.80)	(10%)	3
Van Wagoner Emerging Growth	VWEGX	2/19/99	$17.15	9/22/99	$26.38	$9.23	21%	7
Van Wagoner Emerging Growth	VWEGX	6/8/99	$20.34	9/22/99	$26.38	$6.04	29%	4
First Hand Technology	TVFQX	6/8/99	$49.05	9/22/99	$64.44	$15.39	3%	3
First Hand Technology	TVFQX	7/7/99	$55.23	9/22/99	$64.44	$9.21	16%	3
Warburg Pincus Japan Small Cap	WPJPX	6/8/99	$11.31	9/22/99	$16.96	$5.65	50%	4
Matthews Pacific Tiger	MAPTX	6/8/99	$9.71	9/22/99	$9.94	$0.23	0%	4
Van Wagoner Micro Cap	VVWMCX	8/13/99	$21.56	9/22/99	$23.32	$1.76	8%	1
Rydex Ursa	RYURX	9/24/99	$8.87	11/1/99	$8.83	($0.49)	(5%)	1
Profund Ultra Bear	URPIX	9/28/99	$28.92	11/1/99	$23.35	($5.57)	(19%)	1
Prudent Bear	BEARX	10/8/99	$4.64	11/1/99	$4.22	($0.40)	(8%)	1
Profund Ultra OTC	UOPIX	11/15/99	$56.45	Holding				
Van Wagoner Emerging Growth	VWEGX	11/15/99	$35.11	Holding				
Van Wagoner Micro Cap	VWMCX	11/15/99	$29.52	Holding				
Berger New Generation	BENGX	11/17/99	$31.72	Holding				
Citizens Global	WAGEX	11/17/99	$25.35	Holding				
RS Information Age	RSIFX	11/17/99	$32.38	Holding				
First Hand Technology	TIFQX	11/17/99	$39.37	Holding				

*adjusted for capital gains and dividends distribution

Total of 18 offsets including 7 made for sell signal.

Special Newsletter Offer

Receive the
Al Thomas financial electronic newsletter,
Over My Shoulder
at no cost for one year simply by sending
your name, address
and *e*mail address to:

al@mutualfundmagic.com

Williamsburg Investment Company
830 Waikiki Drive
Merritt Island, Florida 32953

Every one of your friends
should have a copy of this book.

ROBERT ANDERSEN & COMPANY
CERTIFIED PUBLIC ACCOUNTANTS

HIGH POINT TOWER - SUITE 300

400 HIGH POINT DRIVE

COCOA, FLORIDA 32926

(407) 636-1247 - (407) 636-1348 FAX

AMERICAN INSTITUTE OF CPAs

FLORIDA INSTITUTE OF CPAs

July 7, 1999

Mr. Albert W. Thomas
830 Wakiki Drive
Merritt Island, Florida 32953

Re: 1998 Trading Transactions for your Thomas Family LLC Account

Dear Mr. Thomas:

At your request, we have summarized the trading transactions for your Thomas Family LLC trading account at Charles Schwab (Acct. No. x7x3-x7x5) for the period January 1, 1998 through December 31, 1998.

The results of our summary reflected that the account's only investment transactions for the entire year were mutual fund trades with the exception of some minor idle cash investments for very short periods of time throughout the year.

The results of the mutual fund investing in the above mentioned account for calendar year 1998 was a growth in account equity of **39.4%**.

The only other transactions in the account were some cash withdrawals that were taken into consideration in the calculation of the growth in account equity.

Sincerely,

Robert E. Andersen, Jr.

NOTES

NOTES